MASTER QUILTER'S WORKSHOP

ILLUSTRATED GUIDE TO Vintage Quilting™

By Sandra L. Hatch

HOUSE of WHITE BIRCHES
PUBLISHERS
SINCE 1947

Table of Contents

HOUSE of WHITE BIRCHES PUBLISHERS SINCE 1947

ILLUSTRATED GUIDE TO VINTAGE QUILTING is published by House of White Birches, 306 East Parr Road, Berne, IN 46711, telephone (260) 589-4000. Printed in USA. Copyright © 2002 House of White Birches.

RETAILERS: If you would like to carry this pattern book or any other House of White Birches publications, call the Wholesale Department at Annie's Attic to set up a direct account: (903) 636-4303. Also, request a complete listing of publications available from House of White Birches.

Editors: Jeanne Stauffer, Sandra L. Hatch; **Associate Editor:** Dianne Schmidt; **Technical Artist:** Connie Rand; **Copy Editors:** Sue Harvey, Nicki Lehman, Mary Martin; **Graphic Design:** Jessi Butler; **Graphic Artist:** Ronda Bechinski; **Photography:** Jeff Chilcote, Tammy Christian, Kelly Heydinger, Chris Kausch

Vintage Quilting

I love antique quilts. I began my collection in the early 1980s. At that time, I bought a quilt with Flying Geese units that created an unusual railroad-tracks design. I was hooked. It was several years before I purchased my second quilt, but I really did not have a collection until I bought my third quilt. Someone had told me if I had three or more of anything, I could consider it a collection. So, I finally had a collection. Since that time, I have purchased many quilts. Some of them were very expensive, but I couldn't help myself. They seemed to whisper to me when I got close, "Buy me, please!"

Antique quilts can be found in a variety of places and sometimes when you least expect it. One of my favorite quilt finds happened at a local craft store. The owner found out I was involved in quilting and told me about a quilt she had found in the trunk of a friend's car. It was being used as a liner in the trunk. Her friend gave it to her, but she didn't want it anymore, and she wondered if I wanted it. It was a star quilt with some damage, but a perfectly lovely design. I will never forget the story of that quilt or the person who gave it to me.

I have purchased antique quilts, tops and other fabric items at antique shops, flea markets, auctions, through quilt dealers, from private collectors and from e-Bay. If you are interested in looking and are patient, you, too, will find that special quilt.

My collection has become a problem. Whether I choose to store or use my quilts, I have too many. But, I can't bear to part with any of them at the moment. I have several trunks full as well as many being displayed, and yes, some actually being used. As you turn the pages of this book, you will discover how I integrate antique quilts in my home. You will learn how to take care of them and what to look for when purchasing them. I have also included some ideas about how to turn something that isn't finished into something wonderful.

It has been a joy to work with my antique quilts while creating projects for this book. I hope you enjoy trying some of the projects or using the ideas to coordinate with your own quilts.

MEET THE DESIGNER

Sandra L. Hatch has been sewing and making quilts since she was 10 years old. As 4-H club leaders, Sandra's mother and grandmother taught her and others to sew. She grew up with fabric scraps and a treadle sewing machine. Her first quilt was made with crazy patchwork and entered in the state fair. It won a blue ribbon and $1.50 cash.

After 10 years as a middle-school home economics teacher, Sandra became the editor of *Quilt World Omnibook*. Today she edits *Quilt World* and *Quick & Easy Quilting* along with pattern books and hardcover books for House of White Birches. In 1991 she also co-authored *Putting on the Glitz* with Ann Boyce. When she finds the time, Sandra still enjoys sewing, designing and making quilts.

Buying Vintage Quilts, Blocks or Tops

Purchasing vintage or antique quilts, blocks or tops is different than any other kind of spending experience. Educate yourself as much as possible before you begin.

Whether you own lots of antique or vintage quilt blocks, tops or quilts, or you are searching for your first purchase, buying quilts and related items can become an addiction, and an expensive one at that. You should be educated and know as much as possible before you begin the adventure. Even so, many quilt purchases happen because of an immediate connection with the quilt.

Purchased premade templates sold by the pattern company Grandmother Clark's are made from sturdy cardboard and are marked with the block drawing and other important information.

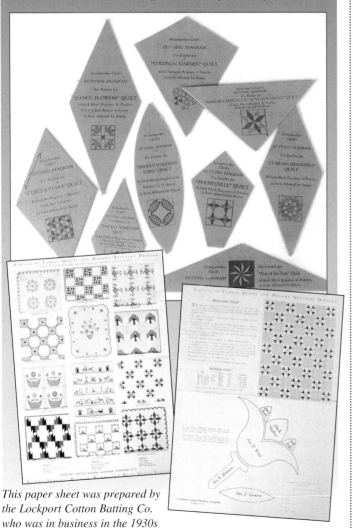

This paper sheet was prepared by the Lockport Cotton Batting Co. who was in business in the 1930s and 1940s. One side of the sheet shows some of their available patterns while the other side shares the pattern for the Holland Tulip.

There are many antique quilt-related items and collecting these items is a whole other topic of discussion. A few such items include old templates, books, tools and art. It would take another book full of information to cover these topics. If you have an opportunity to add some of these items to supplement your quilt collection at a reasonable cost, you might find this an interesting area to explore.

Buying vintage or antique quilts has become too easy for online shoppers. Before the days of computers and shopping sites, the only way to find an antique quilt or related items was good old-fashioned shopping. One could frequent yard sales, antique shops, auctions and antique shows and maybe find a quilt in the desired price range. It took lots of time, and there were many disappointments.

This McCall pattern for the Sunburst and Lone Star quilts was copyrighted in 1933. It cost 35 cents.

I tried all of the above methods of purchasing blocks, tops and quilts. Usually, I was able to find one or two quilts or tops each year that I thought worthy of my hard-earned money and that really wanted to come home with me. They almost spoke to me—"Buy me!"

Today I mostly shop online and at large quilt shows. Online shopping is dangerous; not because of the sellers, but because it is easy to get caught up in the moment. Just like a real, live auction, online auctions, such as e-Bay, have an enormous selection 24 hours a day, seven days a week! It is easy to spend too much. Many of the quilts and tops in this book were purchased online. With only a few exceptions, I have not been disappointed with my purchases or the price I have paid.

When deciding on a quilt purchase, it is good to have some idea of the quilt's age. I know of one example of an online seller who guaranteed a quilt had been made in the 1800s. It was hard to tell from the auction photos. When the quilt arrived, it was evident that it was made after 1980. There was polyester batting visible through holes in the top, and I had some of the fabrics in my own collection just like those used in the quilt. The seller had been deceived when she purchased the quilt at an auction. It was fortunate for my friend that the seller guaranteed the age instead of selling it "as is." The seller refunded the purchase price and accepted the returned quilt.

It is easy to check a seller's reputation on e-Bay. Every buyer has the opportunity to leave feedback about a seller. If you have a bad experience, whether it is in communication, speed of process or information about the item being sold, you can give feedback—positive for a good experience, negative for a bad experience. You can also check on the buyer's reputation based on the feedback. If a seller has had hundreds of transactions with only two or three negative feedbacks, then it is safe to say the seller is probably honest.

I was leery of shopping online in the beginning, but now I find it is much too easy for me to buy. The wonderful thing about it is that if you collect a specific item, you have the world literally at your fingertips, rather than driving hundreds of miles and poking into every nook and cranny. Online shopping is fun and exciting, but the gratification of touching and examining the quilt is delayed until the item arrives.

I have no idea how many antique or vintage quilts I have in my growing collection. It would not be a good idea for me to find out. I do know that each one has given me pleasure, both in the hunt and in the acquisition.

If you are interested in starting a collection, familiarize yourself with some old quilts that you can see in person. Visit museums or quilt shows. Look at the fabrics used. Read all the information given regarding age. This will help you recognize similar fabrics in quilts later. Purchase several books showing antique quilts and read about their history. I have provided a lengthy list of recommended reading. Books created as a result of state quilt searches are wonderful because they show regional themes, and they include the known history of the quilts they share.

FOR YOUR INFORMATION ...

The following is a short list of excellent books that contain historical information and photos of actual fabrics to help you date your vintage quilts.

Quilts from the Civil War by Barbara Brackman

Dating Fabrics A Color Guide 1800–1960 by Eileen Jahnke Trestain

Textile Designs by Susan Meller and Joost Elffers

Worth Doing Twice—Creating Quilts from Old Tops by Patricia J. Morris and Jeannette T. Muir

Collector's Guide to Quilts by Suzy McLennan Anderson

Textiles in America 1650–1870 by Florence Montgomery

America's Printed and Painted Textiles 1600–1900 by Florence Pettit

Clues in the Calico—A Guide to Identifying and Dating Antique Quilts by Barbara Brackman

An Encyclopedia of Pieced Quilt Patterns by Barbara Brackman

Time-Span Quilts—New Quilts from Old Tops by Becky Herdle

Traditional British Quilts by Dorothy Osler

Quilts in America by Patsy and Myron Orlofsky

It is also helpful to purchase a price guide to antique quilts. Though you may never find an exact duplicate to a quilt shown in the guide, you'll be able to relate the age of a quilt to a price range for those of like age, pattern and similar fabrics. This information will help you make informed decisions about purchases.

As you integrate old quilts, blocks or tops into your home, remember that every collector's taste is different. You may confine your collection to a single time period, fabric color or pattern. It helps to have a focus. I love navy-and-white quilts and Flying Geese patterns. I am also drawn to the fabrics from the 1930s. Though I have several in each of these categories, my entire collection really doesn't have a single focus because I buy old quilts for several different purposes.

Many quilts have a history that we may never know. Sometimes the quilt itself can tell you things, such as the talents of the quiltmaker, whether it was made by one person or many, if the maker had enough money to purchase yardage or if scraps of old clothing were used. The quilt can tell you if the maker loved appliqué or piecing. Maybe she loved to quilt, but not appliqué. The quilt can say whether it was used or packed away. It can tell you if it was made for warmth or for decoration. Without speaking, your quilt can tell you quite a story. The story continues with you. Be sure you pass it along to the next owner.

Any factual information you know about your blocks, quilts or tops should be recorded. As mentioned in a later chapter, photos, purchasing information and any other details about pattern, age and history should be saved and passed along with the item to the next owner.

Whatever your reason for purchasing a quilt, be sure you enjoy it and take care of it lovingly.

Repairing Quilts or Quilt Tops

The choice to repair a damaged quilt is yours. Once the decision is made, the goal is to make the repairs as invisible as possible. This can be done by using vintage or reproduction fabrics and methods similar to those used in the construction of the original quilt.

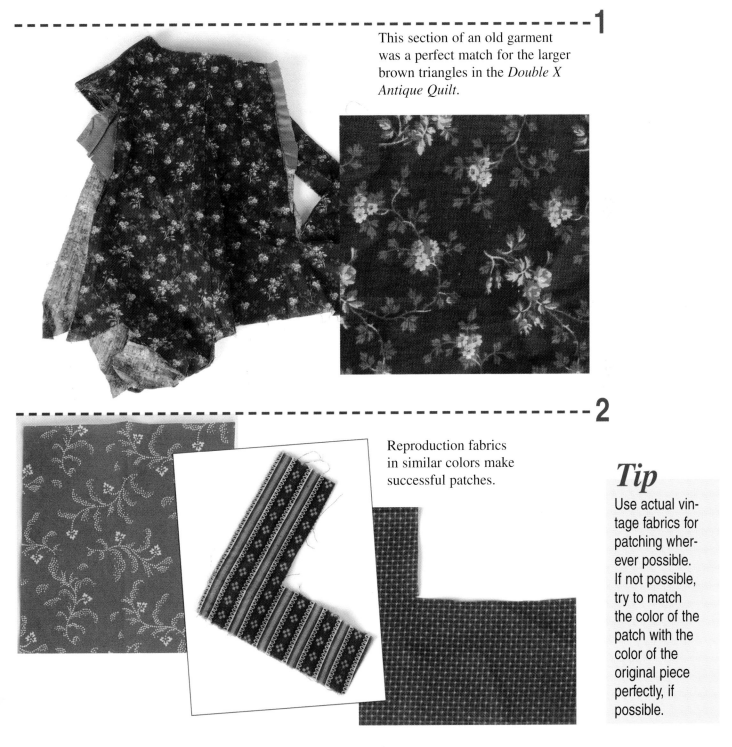

1

This section of an old garment was a perfect match for the larger brown triangles in the *Double X Antique Quilt*.

2

Reproduction fabrics in similar colors make successful patches.

Tip

Use actual vintage fabrics for patching wherever possible. If not possible, try to match the color of the patch with the color of the original piece perfectly, if possible.

3

Remove the damaged fabric patch, picking out thread in seams.

Tip

Look for old quilt tops made with large pieces that cannot be repaired. These may be laundered, taken apart and used to repair quilts of the same era.

4

Place a piece of template plastic on top of the piece to be replaced; trace shape using a pencil.

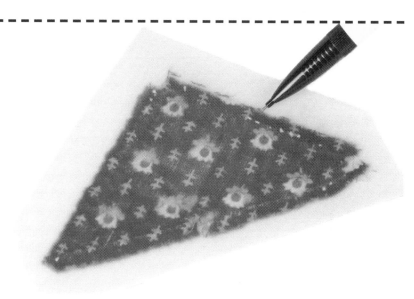

5

Connect lines on the template plastic.

Using a clear ruler with a 1/4" mark, add a seam allowance to the template. Square off pointed ends 1/4" from point.

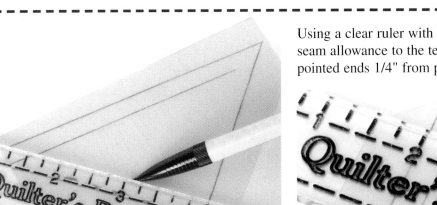

Cut out template on traced line.

Trace the template on the wrong side of the chosen replacement fabric.

Tip

You may eliminate the seam allowance on the template, trace the finished-size template onto the wrong side of the fabric and add a seam allowance all around when cutting the patch.

9 Cut out fabric patch.

Tip

For appliqué repair, apply a new fabric patch on top of the original patch, turning under edges of the new patch along the edges of the original patch as you stitch.

10 Examine the open area to be patched; check to see where patch will tuck inside or be applied on top of original quilt.

11 Remove quilting stitches in the area where new patch will be tucked inside.

Finger-press seam allowance to the wrong side on replacement patch.

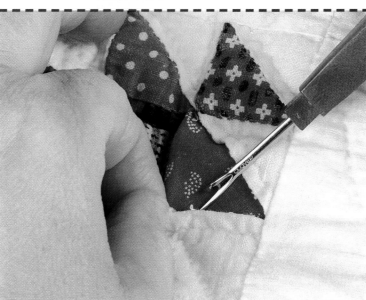

Tuck the new patch under previous finished seams.

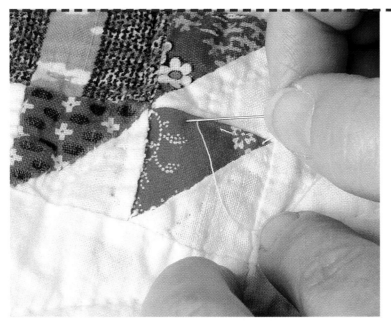

Baste new patch in place.

Tip

Use fabric glue to hold the patch in place on the batting layer while preparing to stitch.

15

Hand-stitch patch in place using thread to match fabric.

16

Hand-quilt using same thread color and placement as in original piece.

Tip

Try to match the size of the replacement quilting stitches to the size of the original stitches. The goal of a good repair job is that on close inspection it would be hard to tell that the quilt had been repaired at all.

17

Photo shows replacement pieces stitched in place.

Christmas Snowball

An old top takes on new life with some replacement blocks and added borders.

PROJECT NOTES

I like my quilts to have borders—even if they are plain fabric strips. To me, no quilt is complete without that frame. Paintings look much better when they are matted and framed, and the same goes for quilts.

The Snowball & Nine-Patch quilt top had no borders. The blocks on the two outside strips were made at a later time with a different red solid fabric that did not exactly match the original fabric.

This old red-and-white Snowball & Nine-Patch quilt top was in fair condition when I purchased it. Upon close inspection, I found several pin-size holes in the top. I also found that the outside blocks on both long sides were made with a different red solid than the inner blocks. I had simply planned to add border strips to this top and have it professionally machine-quilted. It required more attention than I thought.

I began by removing those outside strips. I had some yardage of red solid that was an exact match to the original fabric. I don't know how that happened, but I was very happy. I thought it was a simple matter to make some replacement blocks and add borders. I was wrong again.

As I began the process of measuring the original blocks, I realized that they were not made in any standard or consistent size. They appeared to be 6" x 6" units, but they weren't. Some were 6 1/2" square, while others were smaller or larger. How was I going to be able to make all different size blocks?

The photo shows one of the strips that was removed from the original top because colors did not match exactly.

I had already looked at the backside of the quilt and discovered the seams were less than 1/8" when I took off the wrong-color units. The block pieces were hand-stitched, but the assembled blocks were stitched together by machine. It appeared as if the blocks were made by one person, found

The seams on the backside of the top were less than 1/8" and frayed.

later by another and put together. That would explain the fabrics not matching. The machine stitching was very small, leading me to believe the blocks were stitched together on a treadle machine at the smallest stitch length.

I decided to cut my pieces as if I was making a 6" finished block, but I would sew the seams with a less than 1/8" seam allowance. I hoped that would make the adjustment in size. It worked in some places and not in others. When I finished with my replacement units and added them to the quilt top, I had to stretch in some places and ease in others. This made a quilt top that was not really flat.

I added the borders you see on the quilt, and, of course, those did not work out as they should either. After I got the whole thing pieced, I decided I would wash it. The top was dirty, and maybe the washing and pressing afterward would help a little.

I washed the removed sections to test for colorfastness. I was very surprised that the red did not run. I decided to wash the top in my washing machine on gentle, and then I dried it in my dryer, again on gentle. It took me two hours to cut all the frayed threads on the backside and another hour to iron it using a misting spray bottle.

I patched the holes using fabrics to match the original and some fusible transfer web to make iron-on-patches, which I ironed under the holes on the wrong side.

The quilt top ended up to be very pretty in spite of the fact that seams do not match and all the other obvious problems. The instructions that follow are to piece the quilt as shown in the Placement Diagram. Even though this pattern is the same as the *Snowball & Nine-Patch* quilt on page 116, it has a totally different look and the blocks are a different size. Because the piecing is easy and works up quickly, this makes the perfect type of quilt to make for a holiday decor.

PROJECT SPECIFICATIONS
Quilt Size: 84" x 96"

Block Size: 12" x 12"

Number of Blocks: 42

MATERIALS
- 5 1/4 yards red solid
- 5 1/4 yards muslin
- Backing 88" x 100"
- Batting 88" x 100"
- All-purpose thread to match fabrics
- Cream machine-quilting thread
- Basic sewing supplies and tools, rotary cutter, mat and ruler

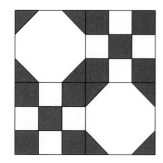

Snowball & Nine-Patch
12" x 12" Block

INSTRUCTIONS

Step 1. Cut 14 strips 6 1/2" by fabric width muslin; subcut each strip into 6 1/2" squares segments for A. You will need 84 A squares.

Step 2. Cut 21 strips 2 1/2" by fabric width red solid; subcut strips into 2 1/2" square segments for B. You will need 336 B squares.

Step 3. Draw a diagonal line from corner to corner on the wrong side of each B square.

Step 4. Place a B square right sides together on one corner of A as shown in Figure 1; stitch on the marked line.

Figure 1
Place a B square right sides together on 1 corner of A.

Step 5. Trim seam to 1/4"; press B to the right side as shown in Figure 2. Repeat on each corner of A to complete an A-B Snowball unit as shown in Figure 3. Repeat for 84 Snowball units; set aside.

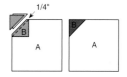

Figure 2
Trim seam to 1/4"; press B to the right side.

Figure 3
Sew B on each corner of A to complete an A-B Snowball unit.

Step 6. Cut 23 strips muslin and 28 strips red solid 2 1/2" by fabric width.

Step 7. Sew a muslin strip between two red solid strips with right sides together along length; press seams toward red solid strips. Repeat for 11 strip sets. Subcut strip sets into 2 1/2" segments as shown in Figure 4; you will need 168 red/muslin/red segments.

Step 8. Sew a red solid strip between two muslin strips with right sides together along length; press seams toward red solid strip. Repeat for six strip sets. Subcut strip sets into 2 1/2" segments, again referring to Figure 4; you will need 84 muslin/red/muslin segments.

Figure 4
Subcut strip sets into 2 1/2" segments.

Figure 5
Join segments to make a Nine-Patch unit.

Step 9. Sew a muslin/red/muslin segment between two red/muslin/red segments to complete a Nine-Patch unit as shown in Figure 5; repeat for 84 Nine-Patch units. Press seams in one direction.

Step 10. Join two Nine-Patch units with two A-B Snowball units to make a block as shown in Figure 6; press seams in one direction.

Step 11. Join six blocks to make a row as shown in Figure 7; repeat for seven rows. Press seams in one direction. Join the rows to complete the pieced center; press seams in one direction.

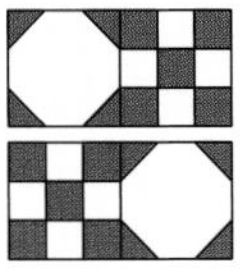

Figure 6
Join 2 Nine-Patch units with 2 A-B Snowball units to make a block.

Figure 7
Join 6 blocks to make a row.

Step 12. Cut and piece two strips each 2 1/2" x 76 1/2" and 2 1/2" x 84 1/2" red solid. Sew the longer strips to opposite long sides and shorter strips to the top and bottom of the pieced center; press seams toward strips.

Step 13. Cut six strips each 2 1/2" by fabric width red solid and muslin; sew a red solid strip to a muslin strip with right sides together along length. Press seams toward red solid strips. Repeat for six strip sets.

Step 14. Subcut strip sets into 2 1/2" segments as shown in Figure 8; you will need 84 segments.

Step 15. Join two segments on short ends as shown in Figure 9; repeat to join 22 segments to make one long strip for side borders; press seams in one direction. Repeat for two side border strips. Repeat with 20 segments for top and bottom border strips.

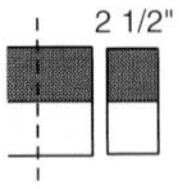

Figure 8
Subcut strip sets into 2 1/2" segments.

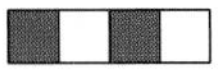

Figure 9
Join 2 segments on short ends.

Step 16. Sew the 22-segment strips to opposite long sides of the pieced center; press seams away from pieced strips. Sew the 20-segment strips to the top and bottom of the pieced center; press seams away from the pieced strips.

Step 17. Cut and piece two strips each 2 1/2" x 84 1/2"

Christmas Snowball
Placement Diagram
84" x 96"

and 2 1/2" x 92 1/2" red solid. Sew the longer strips to opposite sides and shorter strips to the top and bottom of the pieced center; press seams toward strips.

Step 18. Sandwich batting between the completed top and prepared backing piece; pin or baste layers together to hold flat.

Step 19. Quilt as desired by hand or machine. ***Note:*** *The project shown was professionally machine-quilted using cream machine-quilting thread.*

Step 20. Cut nine 2 1/4" by fabric width strips muslin. Join the strips on short ends to make one long strip for binding.

Step 21. Fold binding strip with wrong sides together along length and press. Pin to the quilt top edges with raw edges even. Stitch all around, mitering corners and overlapping ends. Turn binding to the backside; hand-stitch in place to finish. ❖

Double X Antique Quilt

The Double X quilt has led a double life—the top was made in the late 1800s, was probably quilted in the 1980s (polyester batting was not around in the 1800s) and has been repaired in 2000.

PROJECT NOTES

Quilts can lead several lives. This one is a perfect example. Several of the brown fabrics used in the original top have deteriorated over time and have actually almost disappeared. This makes it easy to see that the batting inside is polyester. What I wonder is why the top was not repaired and the bad pieces replaced when it was quilted, probably in the 1970s or 1980s. Could it be that the quilt has been washed since that time, causing the damage? I can't tell and will never know.

Replacing the bad pieces is not simple in this quilt because of the new quilting. To replace the pieces, quilting stitches must be removed, the bad pieces removed entirely and new pieces inserted. The new pieces must be hand-stitched in place, then new quilting added. This takes some time; however, this quilt is worth the work. Only a few of the pieces need to be replaced, and many of the fabrics look almost as good as new.

Because I have swatches of the original old brown prints, my replacement pieces do not show. After I am gone, no one will ever know about this quilt's double life, unless I leave behind written notes about it for its next owners. They won't be able to see the polyester batting. The backing is muslin, so it won't give the age away. It could be sold as an all-original quilt from the 1800s and fetch a high price. Of course, the new owner might not care about that. They might love the quilt no matter what the age, and the price might be worth it.

To reproduce the look of this quilt, gather assorted brown, rust and gold prints for each block. The blocks are all different, but use the same color families, except for the one purple block. I wonder why the quilter chose to make only one block in this color family. Also puzzling is the border fabric. It looks like old fabric, but if new fabric was used, it would seem as if a more appropriate choice could have been made to match the blocks. I like to conjure up reasons for this and ruminate about them. Of course, this is another thing I will never know.

PROJECT SPECIFICATIONS

Quilt Size: 97 3/4" x 97 3/4"

Block Size: 9" x 9"

Number of Blocks: 49

MATERIALS

- 3/4 yard total dark brown prints for A
- 3/4 yard pink tone-on-tone for borders
- 1 1/2 yards total medium brown prints for C
- 1 3/4 yards total rust prints for D
- 7 1/2 yards muslin
- Backing 102" x 102"
- Batting 102" x 102"
- All-purpose thread to match fabrics
- Cream hand-quilting thread
- Basic sewing supplies and tools, rotary cutter, mat and ruler and water-erasable marker or pencil

Double X
9" x 9" Block

INSTRUCTIONS

Note: Because each block has different fabrics, the instructions are to piece one block.

Step 1. Cut one 3 1/2" x 3 1/2" square dark brown print for A.

Step 2. Cut two 3" x 3" squares muslin; cut each square in half on one diagonal to make four B triangles.

Step 3. Sew B to each side of A as shown in Figure 1; press seams away from A.

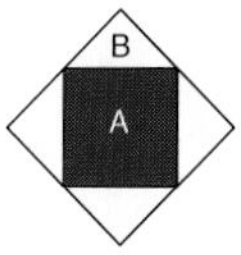

Figure 1
Sew B to each side of A.

Step 4. Cut two 3 7/8" x 3 7/8" squares medium brown print; cut each square in half on one diagonal to make four C triangles.

Step 5. Sew a C triangle to each side of the A-B unit as shown in Figure 2; press seams toward C.

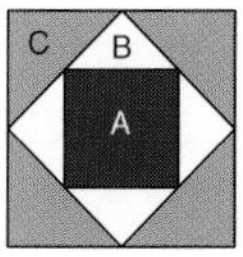

Figure 2
Sew a C triangle to each side of the A-B unit.

Step 6. Cut six 2 3/8" x 2 3/8" squares each muslin and rust print. Cut each square in half on one diagonal to make D triangles. You will need 12 D triangles of each color.

Step 7. Sew a muslin D to a rust print D as shown in Figure 3; repeat for 12 D units.

Figure 3
Sew a muslin D to a rust print D to make a D unit.

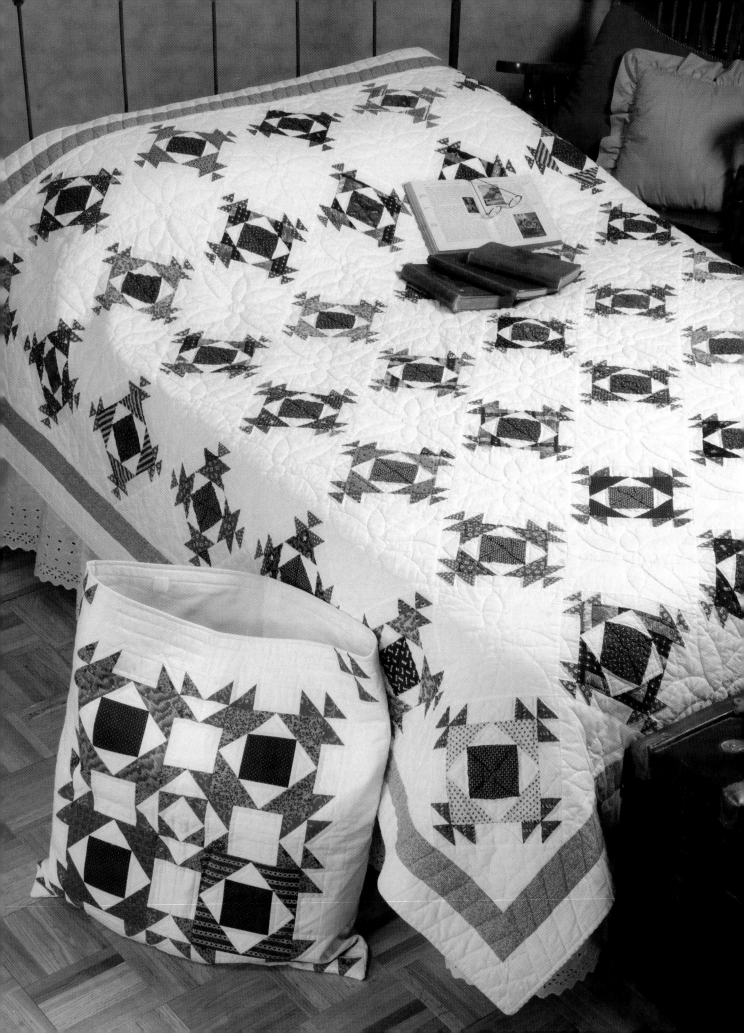

Step 8. Cut four 2" x 3 1/2" rectangles muslin for E.

Step 9. Sew a D unit to opposite short ends of E as shown in Figure 4; repeat for four D-E units.

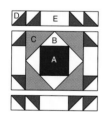

Figure 4
Sew a D unit to opposite short ends of E to make a D-E unit.

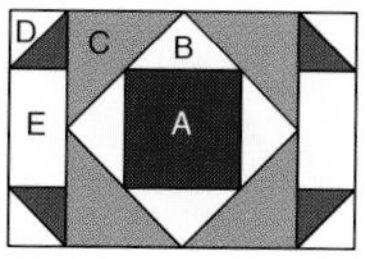

Figure 5
Sew a D-E unit to 2 opposite sides of the A-B-C unit.

Step 10. Sew a D-E unit to two opposite sides of the A-B-C unit as shown in Figure 5; press seams toward the D-E unit.

Step 11. Sew another D unit to each end of the remaining D-E units as shown in Figure 6.

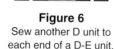

Figure 6
Sew another D unit to each end of a D-E unit.

Step 12. Sew these D-E units to the remaining sides of the pieced unit to complete one block as shown in Figure 7; press seams toward the D-E units. Repeat for 49 blocks.

Figure 7
Sew the other D-E units to the remaining sides of the pieced unit to complete 1 block.

Step 13. Cut 36 muslin squares 9 1/2" x 9 1/2" for F.

Step 14. Cut six 14" x 14" squares muslin; cut each square in half on both diagonals to make 24 G triangles.

Step 15. Cut two 7 1/4" x 7 1/4" squares muslin; cut each square in half on one diagonal to make four H corner triangles.

Step 16. Arrange the blocks with the F squares and H triangles in diagonal rows as shown in Figure 8. Join the blocks and pieces in rows; join the rows to complete the pieced center. Press seams in one direction.

Step 17. Cut and piece two strips each 2 1/2" x 89 3/4" and 2 1/2" x 93 3/4" pink tone-on-tone. Sew the shorter strips to opposite sides and longer strips to the top and bottom of the pieced center; press seams toward strips.

Step 18. Cut and piece two strips each 2 3/4" x 93 3/4"

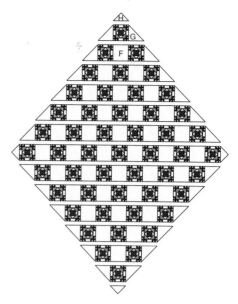

Figure 8
Arrange the blocks with the F squares and G and H triangles in diagonal rows as shown.

and 2 3/4" x 98 1/4" muslin. Sew the shorter strips to opposite sides and longer strips to the top and bottom of the pieced center; press seams toward strips.

Step 19. Mark quilting design given in F, G and H pieces as shown in Figure 9, using water-erasable marker or pencil.

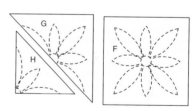

Figure 9
Mark quilting design in F, G and H.

Step 20. Sandwich batting between the completed top and prepared backing piece; pin or baste layers together to hold flat.

Step 21. Quilt as desired by hand or machine. *Note: The quilt shown was hand-quilted in the F, G and H pieces using cream hand-quilting thread and the pattern given. The pieced blocks were hand-quilted 1/4" from seams in the muslin pieces using cream hand-quilting thread.*

Step 22. Cut ten 2 1/4" by fabric width strips muslin. Join the strips on short ends to make one long strip for binding.

Step 23. Fold binding strip with wrong sides together along length and press. Pin to the quilt top edges with raw edges even. Stitch all around, mitering corners and overlapping ends. Turn binding to the backside; hand-stitch in place to finish. ❖

2 1/4" x 97 3/4"
2" x 93 1/4"

2 1/4" x 93 1/4"
2" x 89 1/4"

Double X Antique Quilt
Placement Diagram
97 3/4" x 97 3/4"

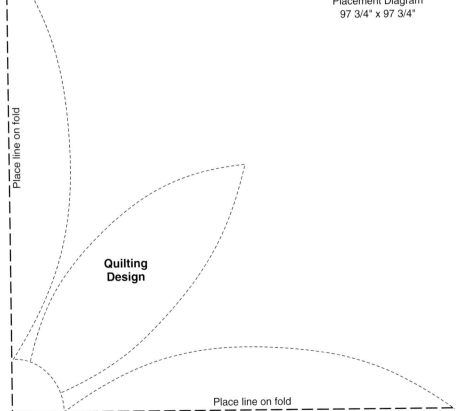

Place line on fold

**Quilting
Design**

Place line on fold

Double X Bag

Make a quilted bag using the pattern from your quilt and store the quilt inside.

PROJECT NOTES

Store your quilt in a matching quilted bag, and you will never have to unfold a quilt to find it; simply look at the quilted bag.

This four-block storage bag can double as a decorative pillow accent when the quilt is inside. When the quilt is in use, a purchased pillow form may be placed inside and then it can be placed on the bed as an accent pillow.

PROJECT SPECIFICATIONS

Bag Size: 24" x 24"

Block Size: 9" x 9"

Number of Blocks: 4

MATERIALS

Double X
9" x 9" Block

- 4 squares dark brown print 3 1/2" x 3 1/2" for A
- 1 strip each gold and rust prints 2 3/8" by fabric width
- 2 squares each 4 different light brown prints 3 7/8" x 3 7/8" for C
- 2 3/4 yards muslin
- 2 batting squares 26" x 26"
- All-purpose thread to match fabrics
- Clear nylon monofilament
- 1 (1" x 3") piece hook-and-loop tape
- Basic sewing supplies and tools, rotary cutter, mat and ruler and water-erasable marker or pencil

INSTRUCTIONS

Step 1. Cut one 3" by fabric width strip muslin; subcut strip into 3" square segments. You will need eight squares. Cut each square in half on one diagonal to make B triangles; you will need 16 B triangles.

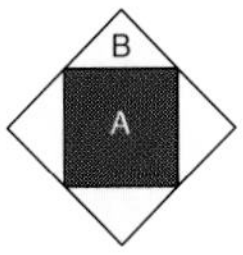

Figure 1
Sew B to each side of A.

Step 2. Sew B to each side of an A square as shown in Figure 1; press seams away from A. Repeat for four A-B units.

Step 3. Cut each C square in half on one diagonal to make four C triangles of each fabric.

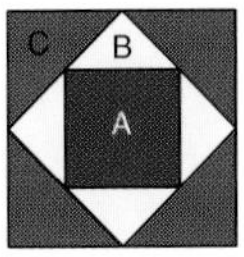

Step 4. Sew a same-fabric C triangle

Figure 2
Sew a C triangle to each side of the A-B unit.

to each side of one A-B unit as shown in Figure 2; press seams toward C. Repeat for four A-B-C units.

Step 5. Cut two 2 3/8" by fabric width strips muslin. Subcut muslin, and rust and gold print strips into 2 3/8" square segments; you will need 15 squares each gold and rust print, and 30 muslin squares. Cut each square in half on one diagonal to make D triangles. You will need 30 D triangles each gold and rust prints, and 60 muslin.

Step 6. Sew a gold print D to a muslin D as shown in Figure 3; repeat for 30 gold/ muslin D units. Sew a rust print D to a muslin D; repeat for 30 rust/muslin D units.

Figure 3
Sew a muslin D to a gold print D to make a D unit.

Step 7. Cut one 3 1/2" by fabric width strip muslin; subcut into 2" segments for E. You will need 16 E rectangles.

Step 8. Sew a gold/muslin D unit to opposite short ends of E as shown in Figure 4; repeat for eight gold/muslin D-E units. Repeat with the rust/muslin D units to make eight rust/muslin D-E units.

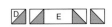

Figure 4
Sew a D unit to opposite short ends of E to make a D-E unit.

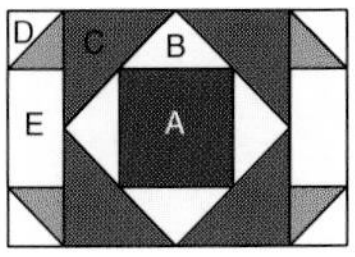

Figure 5
Sew a D-E unit to 2 opposite sides of the A-B-C unit.

Figure 6
Sew another D unit to each end of a D-E unit.

Step 9. Sew a same-fabric D-E unit to two opposite sides of an A-B-C unit as shown in Figure 5; press seams toward the D-E unit. Repeat for all A-B-C units.

Step 10. Sew another same-fabric D unit to each end of the remaining D-E units as shown in Figure 6.

Step 11. Sew these D-E units to the remaining sides of the pieced units to complete four blocks as shown in Figure 7; press seams toward the D-E units.

Step 12. Join the four blocks referring to the Placement Diagram for positioning of blocks; press seams in one direction.

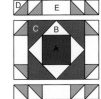

Figure 7
Sew the D-E units to the remaining sides of the pieced unit to complete 1 block.

Double X Bag
Placement Diagram
24" x 24"

Step 13. Cut four 3 1/2" x 18 1/2" strips muslin for G and four 2" x 2" squares muslin for F. Sew a G strip to opposite sides of the pieced center; press seams toward G.

Step 14. Join three rust/muslin D units with F as shown in Figure 8; repeat for four D-F units.

Figure 8
Join 3 rust/muslin D units with F to make a D-F unit.

Figure 9
Sew a D-F unit to each end of the remaining G strips.

Step 15. Sew a D-F unit to each end of the remaining G strips as shown in Figure 9; sew the D-F-G strips to the remaining sides of the pieced center. Press seams toward the D-F-G strips.

Step 16. Cut three squares muslin 24 1/2" x 24 1/2" for lining and backing.

Step 17. Lay the pieced top on one batting square; quilt 1/4" from seams in muslin pieces and through the center of the G strips using clear nylon monofilament in the top of the machine and all-purpose thread in the bobbin. Trim excess batting even with the quilted top.

Step 18. Mark diagonal lines 1" apart on one muslin square using the water-erasable marker or pencil. Lay the marked square on top of the remaining batting square for bag back. Machine-quilt on marked lines using clear nylon monofilament in the top of the machine and all-purpose thread in the bobbin. Trim excess batting even with the muslin back.

Figure 10
Join the muslin back with the quilted front along 1 edge.

Step 19. Join the muslin back with the quilted front along one edge only as shown in Figure 10; press seam open and trim excess batting from seam.

Step 20. Stitch the remaining two muslin squares together on one side; press seam open.

Step 21. Center and stitch the hook side of the hook-and-loop tape to the right-side top edge of one muslin square and the loop side to the opposite side as shown in Figure 11.

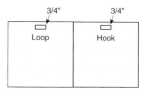

Figure 11
Center and stitch the hook side of the hook-and-loop tape to the right-side top edge of 1 muslin square and the loop side to the opposite side.

Step 22. Place the stitched lining piece right sides together with the top/backing piece and stitch along top edge. Press seam toward lining piece; topstitch along seam on the lining side as shown in Figure 12.

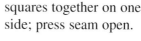

Figure 12
Press seam toward lining piece; topstitch along seam on the lining side.

Step 23. Fold the bag and lining right sides together as shown in Figure 13; stitch along bottom edges and up the long sides, leaving a 6"–8" opening on the lining bottom edge, again referring to Figure 13.

Step 24. Turn right side out through opening and push lining inside the bag. Press along seams and push corners out to make flat. Topstitch along open edge into G pieces using clear nylon monofilament in the top of the machine and all-purpose thread in the bobbin, stitching through the hook-and-loop tape to secure and finish bag. ❖

Figure 13
Fold the bag and lining right sides together; stitch along bottom edges and up the long sides, leaving a 6"–8" opening on the lining bottom edge.

Recycling Old
Quilt Blocks & Tops

*Recycling or repairing old quilt blocks and tops gives one a sense
of accomplishment and a connection to the past and the original stitcher.*

Today we call all our unfinished projects UFOs (unfinished objects). Most quilters have lots of them. They can be unfinished for many reasons: you run out of matching fabric and can't find more; you don't like it after you get the fabrics cut and begin stitching; it was too hard; you got sick. There can be lots of reasons or excuses.

The fact is, you will probably never finish most of these projects unless you set a goal to do so. This might be phrased like a New Year's resolution: "This year I promise to finish one UFO a month." Just like all other resolutions, you are setting yourself up to fail, unless you really mean it.

Don't worry, some day your UFOs will be someone else's treasure. This could happen in 20 years or in 100 years, but one day someone will find your secret stash of UFOs. If they are caring individuals, they won't throw them away as trash, but will find a good home for them with someone who really cares, like me.

Of course, I have my own stash of UFOs, but I find finishing someone else's more fun. I think I am being thrifty—taking something that isn't really useful or pretty as it is and making it into something I can use. I don't feel too much guilt over my own unfinished projects, as I am hoping that long in the future someone else will enjoy resurrecting them as well. It might be fun to leave notes for them with the materials so they will know how much I appreciate their work on my behalf.

This box was found in an attic with a note on the cover "The makings of a quilt." The contents include cut patches, templates and more fabric for some kind of appliquéd flower. No instructions were included, so it is a guess about how these pieces should be used.

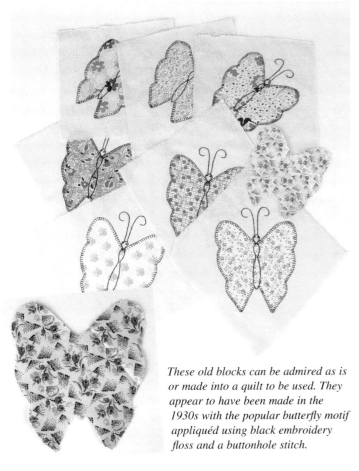

These old blocks can be admired as is or made into a quilt to be used. They appear to have been made in the 1930s with the popular butterfly motif appliquéd using black embroidery floss and a buttonhole stitch.

This box was found with the original McCall's pattern with cut patches. Some of the pieces have been stitched together.

I don't have any such notes with any of my unfinished antique pieces, but I have lots of interesting things. I have a box of cut patches with cardboard templates all cut for a floral appliqué design, but I don't have a pattern. I keep that UFO in a special place and only look at it when I want to. I have a box with partially finished Lone Star units with the original McCall's pattern and cut fabric patches. I have not considered finishing that one. I like looking at it just the way it is.

A friend gave me some tiny pieced star units. She shared these with another of her friends. We were each going to make something from them. I have tried to bring myself

These tiny star shapes need to either be appliquéd to background squares or have background triangles and squares set in—either way, this is not a quick resurrection.

to cut the tiny fill-in squares and triangles it would take to complete the units into a block that I could use to make a small quilt, but every time I look at them, I get nervous. I touch them, think of the special lady who gave them to me, then tenderly place them back in their storage envelope and put them away again.

I have a box of pinwheel blocks that I bought at an American Quilt Study auction. I love the pink plaids mixed with the brown fabrics. I have had those blocks out on a flat surface at least five times and have attempted drawings of different ways to put them together. After an hour of this, each time I pick them up, put them back in their box and put them away until the next time. One day I really will make something with them, but I need the right fabric first.

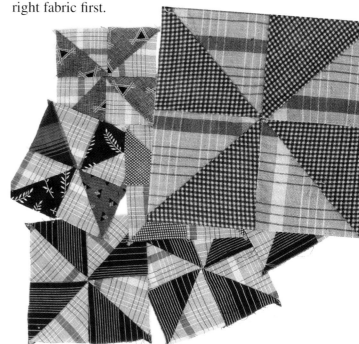

I have lots of antique UFOs. I am slowly working my way into making them into something useful or pretty. Single blocks could be used as the center of a bordered table topper or pillow. Lots of blocks of the same design could be made into a small quilt. Even blocks of different designs and sizes could be combined to make an interesting quilt. There are endless possibilities.

I have 14 of the blue 16" blocks and 13 of the pink blocks which I will someday use to make two different quilts.

This chapter shares several of my resurrected projects. One is now a youth-bed-size quilt for a little girl. I don't remember where I found this piece, but it was a perfect example of how to take an unfinished top and make something really nice from it.

Another project used some poorly pieced blocks which were not uniform in size. I spent some time thinking about what to do with those, and finally I realized that many of the blocks were made with homespun plaids and checks. That fact helped me create the Plaid Mystery Foot-Warmer quilt you see on page 43.

The blocks that I used in the *Star and Crescent Table Cover* (page 38) seemed hopeless. They were poorly pieced to the point of coming apart. They had been stitched together into a top which was uneven and puckered with some torn areas. I loved the design and the blue-and-white fabrics, but I just did not know

what to do with the blocks. Then I decided I would cut the blocks all the same size, even if it meant cutting off the points. The pieced top, as it existed, had points cut off, too, so I really wasn't causing much more damage than there already was.

I removed the worst of the blocks, and from the original 16 I only used nine. This project makes a great centerpiece for my antique oak table. It also has a story to tell about its second life as a repaired quilt.

I love my red-and-white *Christmas Snowball* (page 15). The original top had apparently been handed on to a second person who added a row to each long side; however, the red fabric was not a match so it did not really look right. Also, I thought it needed a border. The finished quilt is still not a masterpiece because the original blocks were pieced without

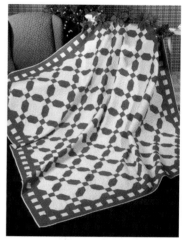

matching seams, but it makes a beautiful Christmas quilt, and no one will ever notice its imperfections.

Old, unfinished projects can have life. They can be finished as they are or changed to fit into a whole new layout. The fun is in finishing something that originally was useless and unattractive.

Don't worry about your own UFOs. Just slip a note into the folds for the next owner with a little bit of information about the project and yourself, so they will feel a real connection to you when they finish your project for you. ❖

Blue Sue Wall Quilt

An old block was recycled as the center of a pastel-colored wall quilt using coordinated reproduction prints.

PROJECT NOTES

A large appliquéd Sunbonnet Sue block created in the 1930s was used as the design focus and center block for this pretty wall quilt. I found the block in a box of things my grandmother bought at a flea market and gave to me many years ago. The pieces were machine-stitched to the muslin background and the details were hand-stitched using black embroidery floss.

The block was originally about 16" square, but I cut it down to 14 1/2" x 14 1/2" to fit in the center of my wall quilt design. I found some reproduction 1930s prints and a blue solid to match and had fun creating a pretty decorative wall quilt from an old block. I have no idea if this block was a leftover block from a quilt, or if the maker made just one block and did not enjoy the process. What I do know is that I am happy with my efforts at taking an old block packed in a box and making it into something useful.

Whether you choose to make your own Sunbonnet block or you have another block, you might like to center it in this setting; it is simple to make a pretty wall quilt with just one block.

PROJECT SPECIFICATIONS

Quilt Size: 29" x 29"

Block Size: 3" x 3" and 14" x 14"

Number of Blocks: 1 large and 12 small

MATERIALS

- 14 1/2" x 14 1/2" square muslin or cream-on-cream print
- 1 fat quarter blue-and-white print
- 1 fat quarter blue solid
- 1/3 yard cream-on-cream print (includes binding)
- 1/3 yard blue floral print
- Backing 33" x 33"
- Batting 33" x 33"
- White all-purpose thread
- 6-strand black embroidery floss
- Blue hand-quilting thread
- 3 (1") white bone rings
- Basic sewing supplies and tools, rotary cutter, mat and ruler and water-erasable marker or pencil

Nine-Patch
3" x 3" Block

Sunbonnet Sue
14" x 14" Block

INSTRUCTIONS

Step 1. Prepare templates for appliqué pieces using full-size pattern given. Trace shapes onto the right side of fabrics as directed on each piece using a water-erasable marker or pencil.

Step 2. Cut out shapes, adding a 1/8"–1/4" seam allowance all around.

Step 3. Turn under edges of each piece along marked line; baste in place.

Step 4. Center the design motif in numerical order on the diagonal of the 14 1/2" x 14 1/2" square muslin or cream-on-cream print. Pin or baste pieces in place.

Step 5. Hand- or machine-stitch pieces in place. *Note: The sample shown was machine-stitched close to the edges of each piece using white all-purpose thread.*

Step 6. Transfer detail lines to dress, bonnet and background square using the water-erasable marker or pencil.

Step 7. Using 2 strands black embroidery floss, straight-stitch ribbon lines on the background. Referring to Figure 1, chain-stitch detail lines on bonnet and dress.

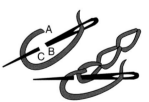

Figure 1
Make a chain stitch as shown.

Step 8. Cut two strips each 1" x 14 1/2" and 1" x 15 1/2" blue floral print. Sew the shorter strips to opposite sides and longer strips to remaining sides; press seams toward strips.

Step 9. Cut five strips blue-and-white print 1 1/2" x 22". Cut two strips 1 1/2" by fabric width cream-on-cream

print. Cut each cream-on-cream print strip into two 1 1/2" x 21" strips.

Step 10. Sew a blue-and-white print strip between two cream-on-cream print strips along length with right sides together; press seams toward darker fabric. Subcut into 1 1/2" segments for A units as shown in Figure 2; you will need 12 A units.

Figure 2
Subcut into 1 1/2" segments for A units.

Figure 3
Subcut into 1 1/2" segments for B units.

Step 11. Sew a cream-on-cream print strip between two blue-and-white print strips along length with right sides together; press seams toward darker fabric. Repeat for two strip sets. Subcut into 1 1/2" segments for B units as shown in Figure 3; you will need 24 B units.

Step 12. Sew an A unit between two B units to make a Nine-Patch block as shown in Figure 4; repeat for 12 blocks. Press seams away from the A units.

Figure 4
Sew an A unit between 2 B units to make a Nine-Patch block.

Step 13. Cut two strips blue solid 3 1/2" x 22"; subcut strips into 3 1/2" square segments for C. You will need 12 C squares.

Step 14. Join two C squares with three Nine-Patch blocks to make a strip as shown in Figure 5; repeat for four strips. Press seams toward C. Sew a C square to opposite ends of two strips as shown in Figure 6; press seams toward C.

Figure 5
Join 2 C squares with 3 Nine-Patch blocks to make a strip.

Figure 6
Sew a C square to opposite ends of 2 strips.

Step 15. Sew the shorter pieced strips to opposite sides and the longer strips to the remaining sides of the pieced center; press seams toward the unpieced strips.

Step 16. Cut four 4 1/2" x 21 1/2" strips blue floral print and four 4 1/2" x 4 1/2" squares blue solid. Sew a blue solid square to opposite ends of two of the strips; press seams toward squares.

Step 17. Sew the shorter strips to opposite sides and the

Blue Sue Wall Quilt
Placement Diagram
29" x 29"

longer strips to the remaining sides of the pieced center; press seams toward strips.

Step 18. Mark the muslin background with 1" crosshatch lines using the water-erasable marker or pencil.

Step 19. Sandwich batting between the completed top and prepared backing piece; pin or baste layers together to hold flat.

Step 20. Hand-quilt on marked lines, around appliquéd shapes, in the ditch of seams between border strips and Nine-Patch and C seams or as desired using blue hand-quilting thread.

Step 21. When quilting is complete, trim batting and backing even with quilt top; remove pins or basting.

Step 22. Cut three 2 1/4" by fabric width strips cream-on-cream print for binding. Join strips on short ends to make one long strip as shown in Figure 7. Trim seams; press. Fold strip with wrong sides together along length; press.

Figure 7
Join strips on short ends to make 1 long strip.

Step 23. Stitch binding strip to quilt top with raw edges even, mitering corners and overlapping ends. Turn binding strip to the backside; hand-stitch in place to finish.

Step 24. Hand-stitch a 1" white bone ring to the top corner and two side corners to hang. ❖

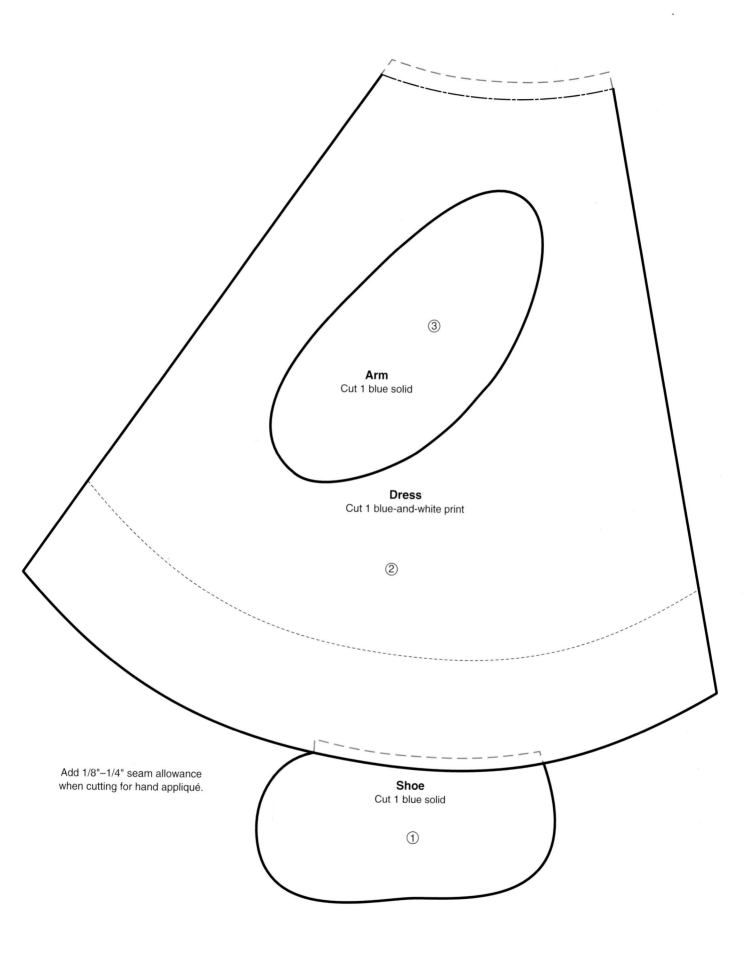

Arm
Cut 1 blue solid

Dress
Cut 1 blue-and-white print

③

②

Add 1/8"–1/4" seam allowance
when cutting for hand appliqué.

Shoe
Cut 1 blue solid

①

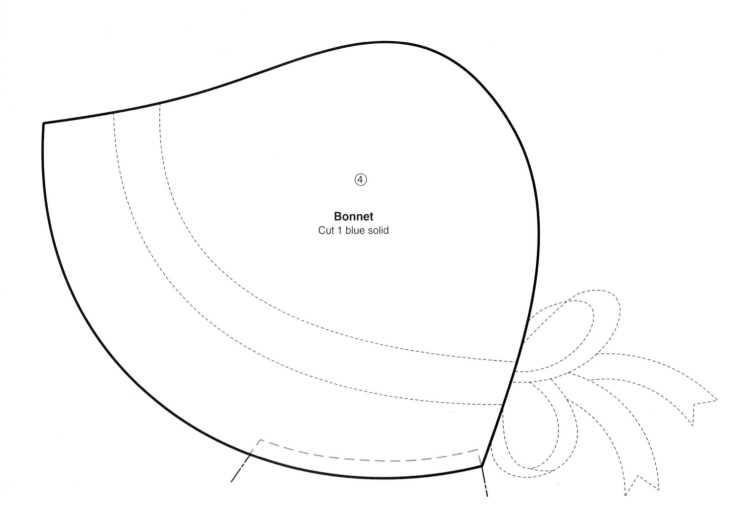

④

Bonnet
Cut 1 blue solid

Lavender Sue

Antique blocks were magically changed when used in a whole new setting.

PROJECT NOTES

The blocks used to make this pretty girl's quilt were resurrected from an old top. The original top shown in the photo had the same purple gingham sashing strips as was used on the dresses. It appears that the original maker ran out of the fabric and never finished the quilt.

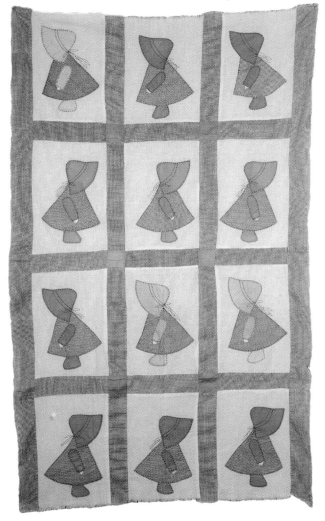

The original quilt did not have any extra fabric to create strips for the top and bottom. It was left in this unfinished state.

There was some damage in the form of stains and rips on the original sashing. I am not sure how that could happen to a quilt that was never used, but it was in sad condition.

I thought I might try to finish it as the original maker intended and looked for some tiny purple gingham to closely match the original. I had no luck. I decided to take the entire top apart and start over.

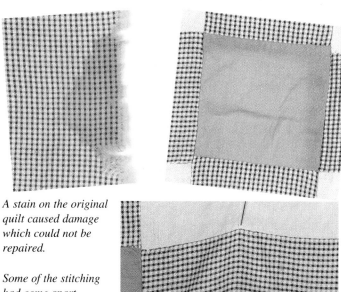

A stain on the original quilt caused damage which could not be repaired.

Some of the stitching had come apart between the seams.

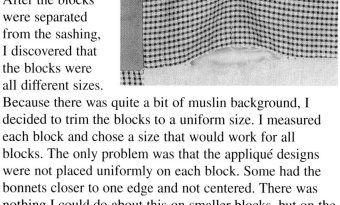

After the blocks were separated from the sashing, I discovered that the blocks were all different sizes. Because there was quite a bit of muslin background, I decided to trim the blocks to a uniform size. I measured each block and chose a size that would work for all blocks. The only problem was that the appliqué designs were not placed uniformly on each block. Some had the bonnets closer to one edge and not centered. There was nothing I could do about this on smaller blocks, but on the larger blocks, I trimmed the excess muslin so that the design was more or less centered. I trimmed all blocks to 8 1/2" x 11 1/2".

Because so many fabric companies are printing reproduction fabrics, I was able to find enough lavender fabrics to create sashing strips bordered with a lavender solid that matched the blocks. In the beginning I planned to use the sashing strips I removed from the original in the pieced strips. The color was not suitable when combined with the other fabrics I had chosen, so I left that out.

The resulting quilt is charming. It is perfect for a little girl's smaller bed.

I do wonder why the original maker did not finish this little

quilt. I would guess the top was made in the 1930s era considering the color and fabrics used. The muslin was not good quality, but rather thin and cut off-grain. Regardless, I am happy with my resurrected quilt. It will make a perfect cover for my granddaughter's bed at Grammie's house.

PROJECT SPECIFICATIONS
Quilt Size: 46" x 70"

Block Size: 8" x 11"

Number of Blocks: 12

MATERIALS
- 1/4 yard lavender print
- 1/4 yard large lavender check
- 1/4 yard small lavender check
- 1/4 yard lavender plaid
- 1/4 yard purple solid
- 1/2 yard purple gingham
- 1 yard lavender-and-white dot
- 1 1/8 yards muslin
- 2 yards lavender solid
- Backing 50" x 74"
- Batting 50" x 74"
- Neutral color all-purpose thread
- Lavender machine- and hand-quilting threads
- Rust 6-strand embroidery floss
- Basic sewing supplies and tools, rotary cutter, mat and ruler

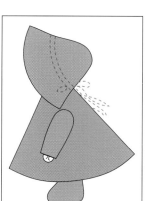

Lavender Sue
8" x 11" Block

INSTRUCTIONS
Step 1. Cut 12 rectangles muslin 8 1/2" x 11 1/2"; fold and crease to find the center of each block.

Step 2. Prepare templates for each appliqué shape using the full-size patterns given. Cut as directed on each piece, adding a 1/8"–1/4" seam allowance all around when cutting.

Step 3. Turn under the seam allowance on each piece; baste in place.

Step 4. Center one motif in numerical order on an 8 1/2" x 11 1/2" muslin rectangle using the crease lines on the rectangle and the X center mark on the motif as guides; pin or baste in place.

Step 5. Fold a muslin circle in half on the marked line with wrong sides together. Hand-stitch a line of gathering stitches along the rounded edge and pull to gather as shown in Figure 1. Tuck the gathered hand piece inside the bottom edge of the sleeve; baste in place.

Figure 1
Gather circle hand piece as shown.

Step 6. Transfer detail lines marked on and around the appliqué motif to the fabrics using the water-erasable marker or pencil.

Step 7. Using 3 strands rust embroidery floss, stitch each piece in place with close, straight stitches referring to Figure 2. Repeat on detail lines as marked to complete one block; repeat for 12 blocks.

Step 8. Cut three strips each lavender print, lavender-and-white dot, large lavender check and lavender plaid 2 1/2" by fabric width. Cut two strips small lavender check 2 1/2" by fabric width.

Step 9. Join one strip of each fabric with right sides together along length to make a five-strip section; press seams in one direction; repeat for two five-strip sections. Repeat with the remaining four strips to make a four strip section; press.

Step 10. Subcut each strip set into 2 1/2" segments as shown in Figure 3. You will need 15 four-unit sections and 21 five-unit sections.

Step 11. Join seven five-unit sections to make a long strip; remove three segments from the end of the strip as shown in Figure 4. Repeat for four strips.

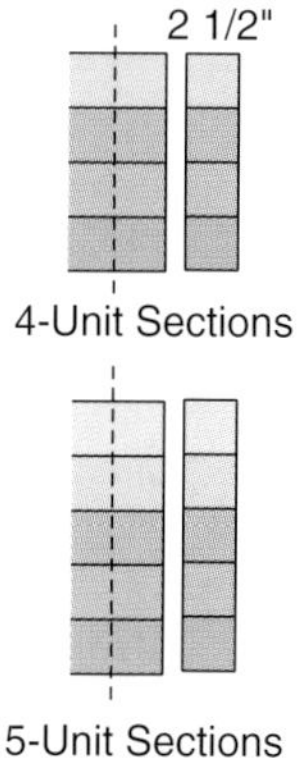

Step 12. Cut eight 1 1/2" x 64 1/2" strips lavender solid along the length of

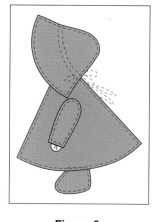

Figure 2
Stitch each piece in place with close, straight stitches.

2 1/2"

4-Unit Sections

5-Unit Sections

Figure 3
Subcut each strip set into 2 1/2" segments.

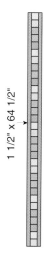

1 1/2" x 64 1/2"

Figure 4
Join seven 5-unit sections to make a long strip; remove 3 segments from the end of the strip.

Figure 5
Sew a 1 1/2" x 64 1/2" lavender solid strip to opposite long sides of each strip.

the fabric. Sew a strip to opposite long sides of each strip with right sides together as shown in Figure 5; press seams toward lavender solid strips.

Step 13. Cut 30 strips lavender solid 1 1/2" x 8 1/2". Sew a strip to opposite sides of each four-unit section as shown in Figure 6.

1 1/2" x 8 1/2"

Figure 6
Sew a 1 1/2" x 8 1/2" strip to opposite sides of each 4-unit section.

Step 14. Join four blocks with five four-unit sections to make a vertical row as shown in Figure 7; repeat for three rows.

Step 15. Join the rows with the previously pieced long strips, beginning and ending with a pieced strip; press seams toward strips.

Step 16. Cut and piece two strips each lavender-and-white dot 3 1/2" x 40 1/2" and 3 1/2" x 70 1/2". Sew the shorter strips to the top and bottom and longer strips to opposite sides of the pieced center; press seams toward strips.

Step 17. Sandwich batting between the completed top and prepared backing piece; pin or baste layers together to hold flat.

Step 18. Quilt as desired by hand or machine. *Note: The quilt shown was hand-quilted around each appliqué motif and in the ditch of seams using lavender hand-quilting thread. The borders were machine-quilted using lavender machine-quilting thread.*

Step 19. Cut six 2 1/4" by fabric width strips lavender solid. Join strips on short ends to make one long strip for binding.

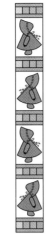

Figure 7
Join 4 blocks with five 4-unit sections to make a vertical row.

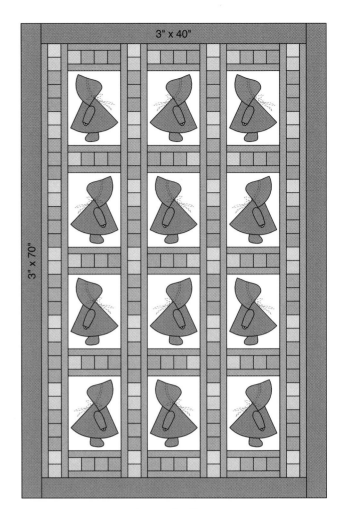

Lavender Sue
Placement Diagram
46" x 70"

Step 20. Fold binding strip with wrong sides together along length and press. Pin to the quilt top edges with raw edges even. Stitch all around, mitering corners and overlapping ends. Turn binding to the backside; hand-stitch in place to finish. ❖

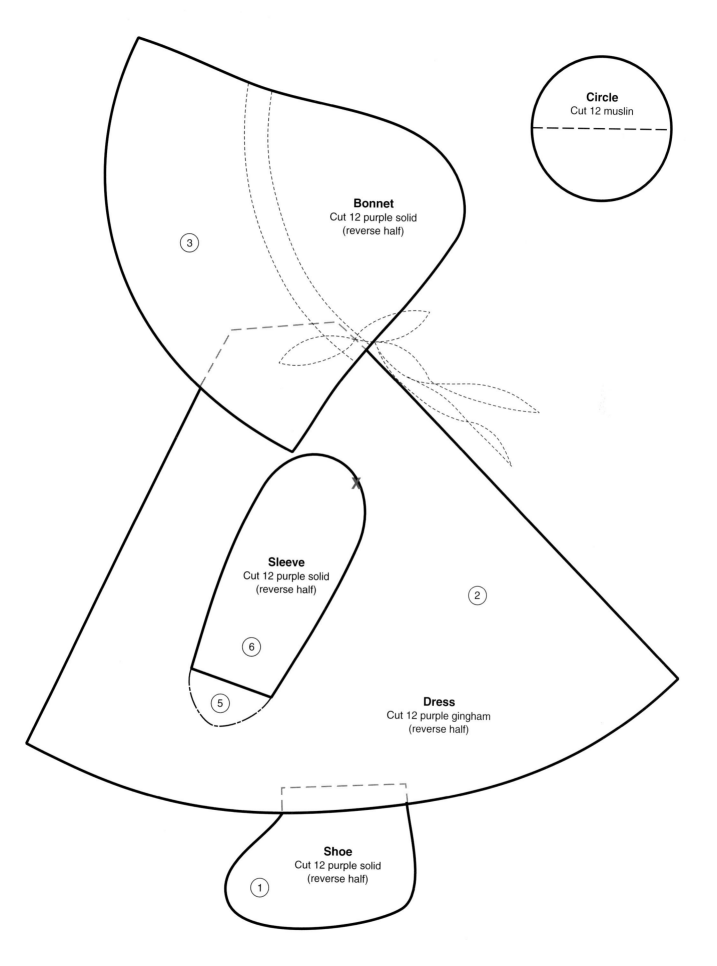

Circle
Cut 12 muslin

Bonnet
Cut 12 purple solid
(reverse half)

③

Sleeve
Cut 12 purple solid
(reverse half)

②

⑥

Dress
Cut 12 purple gingham
(reverse half)

⑤

Shoe
Cut 12 purple solid
(reverse half)

①

Star & Crescent Table Cover

The Star & Crescent pattern is difficult to piece—accuracy is very important in the curved, set-in seams.

PROJECT NOTES

I purchased the original Star & Crescent top from an online auction. It looked very pretty in the photo. The block was interesting, and it was made in my favorite color combination—navy blue and white.

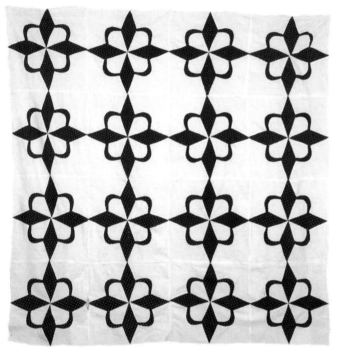

The original quilt top looks good from a distance, but close inspection reveals missing points, poor center matches, unstitched seams and more.

The seams are frayed with inconsistent stitching.

When I received the top, I was not disappointed when I first examined it, as I had not paid very much for it and thought I could use it as it was. Upon closer inspection, I found that it was in terrible condition. The seams were frayed, the centers of the blocks did not meet to make points, the edge points were lost in putting it together and the white outside pieces were not square. I decided to take the top apart.

After I got the blocks separated, I really did not know what to do with them. They needed to be made a consistent size, which meant the points on the outside edges would be cut off even more than they already were. It was impossible to take them apart and restitch them because the seams inside were frayed and in some cases almost gone.

I selected four of the best blocks and decided to join them with some sashing strips, hoping that the sashing would hide or at least take the eye away from the block imperfections.

These blocks show the poor piecing in the block center and the points missing on the edges.

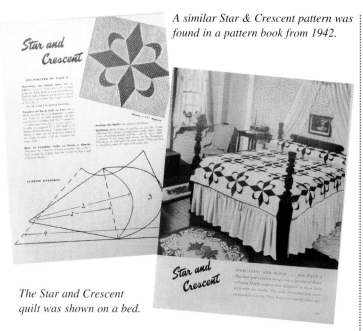

A similar Star & Crescent pattern was found in a pattern book from 1942.

The Star and Crescent quilt was shown on a bed.

Because the blocks were in such bad condition, I did not feel the need to do much quilting on the finished project. This would be a useful table cover, not an heirloom.

I still love the pattern, and the color combination looks wonderful, even with all the imperfections. The instructions are given to piece one block and to make the project as shown. If you would like to make a 75" x 105" quilt with 35 blocks (five by seven) without borders, the materials needed are listed in parentheses.

I found a similar Star & Crescent pattern in *Quilts,* an old pattern book copyrighted in 1942 by The Spool Cotton Co. The quilt shown was made using navy-and-white dot. The book sold for 10 cents.

PROJECT SPECIFICATIONS
Table Cover Size: 44" x 44"
Quilt Size: 75" x 105"
Block Size: 15" x 15"
Number of Blocks: 4 (35)

MATERIALS
- 3/4 yard navy-and-white small dot (7 yards)
- 1 3/8 yards navy-and-white large dot
- 1 1/2 yards white solid (11 yards)
- Backing 48" x 48" (79" x 109")
- Batting 48" x 48" (79" x 109")
- White all-purpose thread
- White hand-quilting thread
- Navy and white machine-quilting thread
- Basic sewing supplies and tools, rotary cutter, mat and ruler

Star & Crescent
15" x 15" Block

INSTRUCTIONS

Step 1. Prepare templates using pattern pieces given; cut as directed for one block. Repeat for four (35) blocks.

Figure 1
Sew A to B.

Step 2. To piece one block, sew A to B as shown in Figure 1; repeat for four units.

Step 3. Join the four A-B units with C as shown in Figure 2.

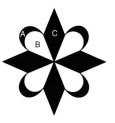

Figure 2
Join 4 A-B units with C.

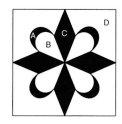

Figure 3
Set in the D pieces to complete 1 block.

Step 4. Set in the D pieces to complete one block as shown in Figure 3; repeat for four (35) blocks.

Step 5. Cut one 15 1/2" by fabric width strip navy-and-white large dot; subcut into 2 1/2" segments for E sashing pieces. You will need 12 E pieces.

Step 6. Cut one 2 1/2" by fabric width strip white solid; subcut into 2 1/2" square segments for F; you will need nine F squares.

Step 7. Join two pieced blocks with three E pieces to make a block row as shown in Figure 4; repeat for two block rows. Press seams toward E.

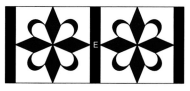

Figure 4
Join 2 pieced blocks with 3 E pieces to make a block row.

Step 8. Join two E pieces with three F squares to make a sashing row as shown in Figure 5; press seams toward E.

Figure 5
Join 2 E pieces with 3 F squares to make a sashing row.

Step 9. Join the block rows with the sashing rows to complete the pieced center; press seams toward sashing rows.

Step 10. Cut and piece four 1 1/2" x 46" strips white solid and four 3 1/2" x 46" strips navy-and-white large dot.

Step 11. Sew a white solid strip to a navy-and-white large dot strip with right sides together along length; press seams toward darker fabric. Repeat for four strip sets.

Step 12. Center and sew a strip to each side of the pieced center, mitering corners; press seams toward strips. Trim excess at mitered corners and press seams open to complete the top.

Step 13. Sandwich batting between the completed top and prepared backing piece; pin or baste layers together to hold flat.

Step 14. Quilt as desired by hand or machine. *Note: The quilt shown was hand-quilted in the ditch of block seams with hand-quilting thread to match fabrics. The border and sashing strips were machine-quilted using machine-quilting thread to match fabrics.*

Step 15. Cut five (nine) 2 1/4" by fabric width strips navy-and-white large dot (navy-and-white small dot). Join the strips on short ends to make one long strip for binding.

Step 16. Fold binding strip with wrong sides together along length and press. Pin to the quilt top edges with raw edges even. Stitch all around, mitering corners and overlapping ends. Turn binding to the backside; hand-stitch in place to finish. ❖

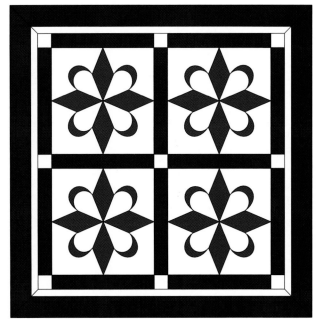

Star & Crescent Table Cover
Placement Diagram
44" x 44"

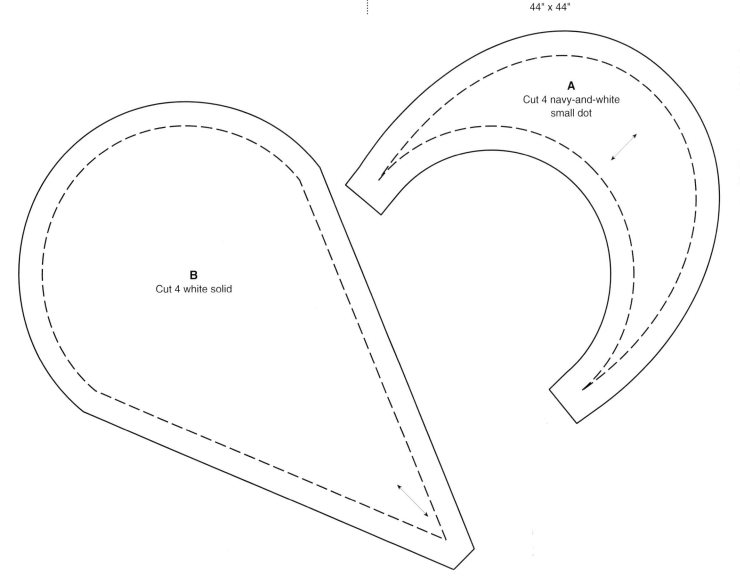

A
Cut 4 navy-and-white
small dot

B
Cut 4 white solid

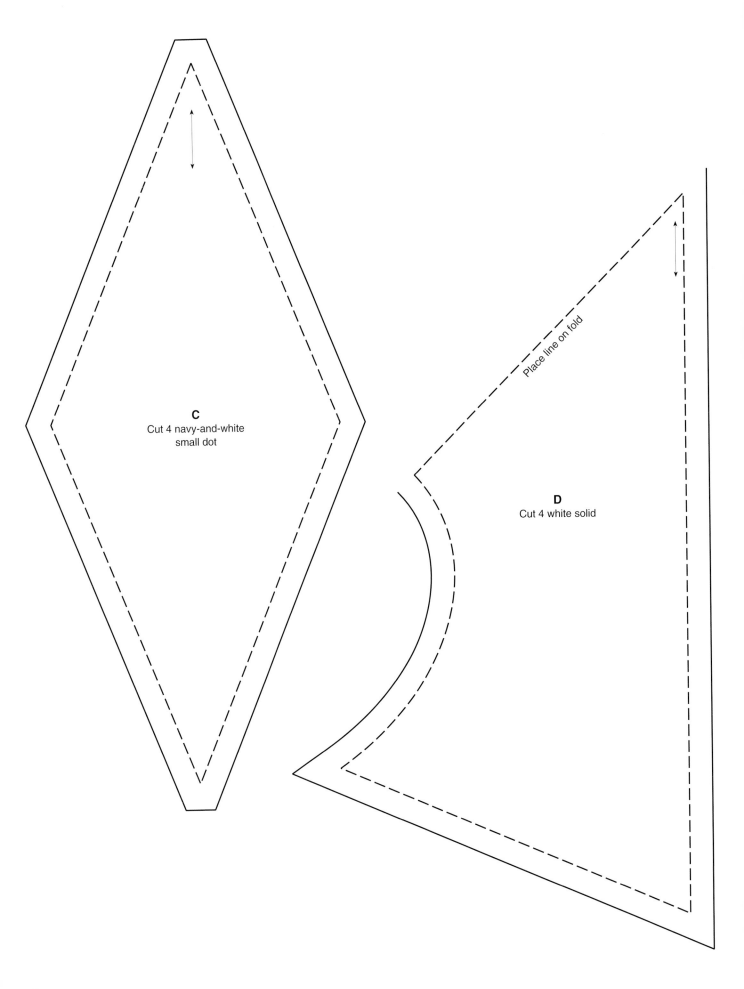

C
Cut 4 navy-and-white
small dot

Place line on fold

D
Cut 4 white solid

Plaid Mystery Foot Warmer

A collection of old blocks was recycled to make this quilted foot warmer.

These blocks were not selected for use because they were not of similar color to those chosen for the project.

PROJECT NOTES

I had a collection of about 20 blocks in the same pattern, but they were not all the same size. Some were at least 1" larger than others. They were not well made. The seams were inconsistent in size and only 1/8" or less in many cases. The colors of the blocks were a mixture with no apparent color scheme. In other words, these blocks were not really useful to complete a quilt.

This very busy block uses a piece which needed to be pieced to fit the template. No attempt was made to match the fabric piecing.

While trying to decide what to do with them, I realized that many of the blocks were made with plaids. I chose 10 of the plaid blocks to create this foot warmer.

To make the blocks a consistent size, I added 2"-wide muslin strips to the sides of each one. Then I trimmed them all to 11 1/2". Even though some blocks had wider muslin strips than others, they were the same overall size and could be used in a project.

I searched through my fabric collection and found some homespun sample cuts, which I thought would be perfect

with these blocks. A few of the large checks were even close to those used in the blocks.

The resulting quilt is a strange size, but fits perfectly across the foot of a bed. It can be used as a decorator accent or as a foot warmer for those people who always have cold feet.

PROJECT SPECIFICATIONS

Quilt Size: 79" x 31"

Block Size: 9" x 9"

Number of Blocks: 10

MATERIALS

- 1 yard total light prints and stripes for block background
- 10 squares 14" x 14" plaids or checks for block design
- 11 strips assorted homespuns 1 1/2" x 42"
- 1 yard green plaid
- 1 1/3 yards muslin
- Backing 83" x 35"
- Batting 83" x 35"
- Neutral color all-purpose thread
- Clear nylon monofilament
- Cream machine-quilting thread
- Basic sewing supplies and tools, rotary cutter, mat and ruler

INSTRUCTIONS

Piecing One Block

Step 1. Cut one square 3 1/2" x 3 1/2" background fabric for A.

Step 2. Cut twelve 2" x 2" squares plaid or check for B; draw a diagonal line from corner to corner on the wrong side of each B square.

Step 3. Place a B square right sides together on one corner of A as shown in Figure 1; stitch on the marked line.

Step 4. Trim seam to 1/4" and press B to the right side as

Plaid Mystery
9" x 9" Block

Figure 1
Place a B square right sides together on 1 corner of A; stitch on the marked line.

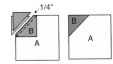

Figure 2
Trim seam to 1/4" and press B to the right side.

Figure 3
Repeat on each corner of A to make an A-B unit.

shown in Figure 2; repeat on each corner of A to make an A-B unit as shown in Figure 3.

Step 5. Cut eight 2" x 2" squares background fabric for C and four 2" x 3 1/2" rectangles plaid or check for D.

Step 6. Sew D to opposite sides of the A-B unit; press seams toward D. Sew a C square to each short end of the remaining D pieces; press seams toward C. Sew a C-D unit to the remaining sides of the A-B unit as shown in Figure 4.

Figure 4
Sew a C-D unit to the remaining sides of the A-B unit.

Step 7. Cut four 2" x 3" rectangles background for E.

Step 8. Sew marked B squares to two corners of E as in Steps 3 and 4 referring to Figure 5 to complete one B-E unit; repeat for four B-E units.

Figure 5
Sew marked B squares to 2 corners of E to complete 1 B-E unit.

Step 9. Cut four 2 3/8" x 2 3/8" squares each background and plaid or check; cut each square in half on one diagonal to make F triangles. You will need eight F triangles each background and plaid or check fabrics.

Step 10. Sew a background F to a plaid or check F with right sides together on the diagonal to make an F unit as shown in Figure 6; press seams toward darkest fabric. Repeat for eight F units.

Figure 6
Make an F unit as shown.

Figure 7
Sew an F unit to opposite ends of each B-E unit.

Step 11. Sew an F unit to opposite ends of each B-E unit as shown in Figure 7; press seams toward F units. Sew a B-E-F unit to opposite sides of the A-B-C-D unit as shown in Figure 8; press seams toward the A-B-C-D unit.

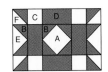

Figure 8
Sew a B-E-F unit to opposite sides of the A-B-C-D unit.

Step 12. Sew C to each end of the remaining B-E-F units and sew to the remaining sides of the pieced unit

to complete one block as shown in Figure 9; press seams toward the A-B-C-D unit. Repeat for 10 blocks.

Step 13. Cut one strip muslin 9 1/2" by fabric width; subcut into 1 1/2" segments for G. You will need 20 G strips. Sew a strip to opposite sides of each pieced block; press seams toward strips.

Step 14. Cut one strip muslin 11 1/2" by fabric width; subcut into 1 1/2" segments for H; you will need 20 H strips. Sew an H strip to the remaining sides of each pieced block referring to Figure 10; press seams toward strips.

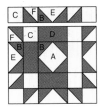

Figure 9
Sew C to each end of the remaining B-E-F units and sew to the remaining sides of the pieced unit to complete 1 block.

Figure 10
Sew G and H to the sides of a pieced block.

Completing Quilt

Step 1. Cut each 1 1/2" x 42" strip homespun in half to make two 1 1/2" x 21" strips of each fabric.

Step 2. Join 11 fabric strips with right sides together along length to make a strip set; press seams in one direction; repeat for two strip sets, changing the placement of fabrics in each strip.

Step 3. Subcut strip sets into 3 1/2" segments as shown in Figure 11; you will need 12 pieced segments.

Step 4. Join five blocks with six pieced segments to make a row as shown in Figure 12; repeat for two rows. Press seams toward muslin strips.

Figure 11
Subcut strip sets into 3 1/2" segments.

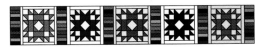

Figure 12
Join 5 blocks with 6 pieced segments to make a row.

Step 5. Cut two 3 1/2" by fabric width strips muslin; subcut into 3 1/2" square segments for J. You will need 18 J squares.

Step 6. Cut two 11 1/2" by fabric width strips green plaid; subcut into 3 1/2" segments for K. You will need 15 K strips.

Step 7. Join six J squares with five K strips to make a sashing row as shown in Figure 13; repeat for three rows. Press seams toward K.

Figure 13
Join 6 J squares with 5 K strips to make a sashing row.

Step 8. Join the block rows with the sashing rows; press seams toward the sashing rows.

Step 9. Cut two 3 1/2" x 31 1/2" strips green plaid; sew a strip to opposite short ends to complete the pieced top. Press seams toward strips.

Step 10. Sandwich batting between the completed top and prepared backing piece; pin or baste layers together to hold flat.

Step 11. Quilt as desired by hand or machine. *Note: The quilt shown was machine-quilted in the ditch of seams using clear nylon monofilament in the top of the machine and all-purpose thread in the bobbin. Cream machine-quilting thread was used to quilt 3/8" from seams on the sashing rows.*

Step 12. When quilting is complete, trim batting and backing even with quilt top; remove pins or basting.

Step 13. Cut six 2 1/4" by fabric width strips muslin for

Plaid Mystery Foot Warmer
Placement Diagram
79" x 31"

binding. Join strips on short ends to make one long strip as shown in Figure 14. Trim seams; press. Fold strip with wrong sides together along length; press.

Step 14. Stitch binding strip to quilt top with raw edges even, mitering corners and overlapping ends. Turn binding strip to the backside; hand-stitch in place to finish. ❖

Figure 14
Join strips on short ends to make 1 long strip.

SQUARING UP OLD BLOCKS

If you have some blocks that are not accurately stitched and you would like to use them in a project, it is easy to salvage them with borders.

Step 1. Measure all the blocks.

Step 2. Choose a fabric to border the blocks that will coordinate with all the blocks.

Step 3. Cut 2" by fabric width strips of the chosen fabric as needed.

Step 4. Sew a strip to one side of one block; press seam toward strip. Trim the strip even with the block using a rotary cutter and ruler as shown in Figure 15.

Figure 15
Trim the strip even with the block.

Step 5. Sew a strip to opposite sides of the block; press and trim. Repeat on the remaining sides of the block. Repeat on all the blocks.

Step 6. Measure the smallest block; choose a finished size at least 1" larger than this block. *Note: The blocks used in the project shown ranged in size from 9"–10". The bordered blocks were trimmed to 11 1/2" x 11 1/2".*

Step 7. Trim the bordered blocks to the chosen size, centering the block when cutting to keep the width of the muslin uniform on all sides. *Note: The blocks used for the sample were not square, so the muslin strips are wider on one end than the other on some blocks.*

Step 8. Use the bordered blocks to create a quilt with sashing strips or as desired.

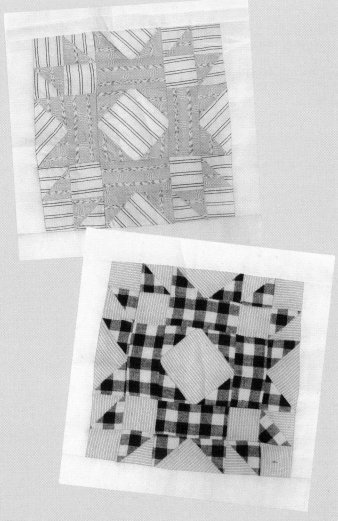

These two blocks have added muslin borders which have been trimmed to make blocks a uniform size for use in a project.

Caring For Vintage Quilts or Quilt Tops

If you are a quilt collector, you have a responsibility to take care of your collection. Whether your collection consists of simple tops that may have been stored away for years, or well-loved quilts that are ragged from use, or masterpiece heirlooms in mint condition, they require some special care.

CLEANING

I have read many articles about quilt care, and there are varying opinions regarding the subject. To wash or not to wash is the major point of contention. There are experts who say that an antique quilt or top should not be washed, no matter what. They feel the dirt and other stains are considered part of the quilt's history, and it is too much of a gamble to take a chance on causing more damage during the cleaning process.

Will the quilt or top be used on a bed, hung on a wall or displayed on a rack? If it will actually be used, smells and dirt are not acceptable choices. If it will be displayed, cleaning might not be necessary. A good airing in fresh, clean air might be enough to get rid of smells. If you simply can't live with a soiled quilt or top and want to wash it, you will find differing opinions among experts.

Almost all conservators agree that dust may be vacuumed from a quilt using a cloth over the cleaning end of the vacuum hose. If you choose this method, be sure your hose attachment and the cloth are clean. The quilt or top can be laid out on a bed where all areas can be reached. Turn the quilt over to reach both sides.

For more serious stains or soiling, washing or dry cleaning are considered. Dry cleaning uses chemicals and is actually not a dry process. One book I read recommended dry cleaning, and the author stated that she had used this process with great success. Personally, I would rather not trust a dry cleaner with one of my quilts, never mind the chemical consideration.

Washing any antique quilt or top requires extreme care. Before making a decision to wash, answer the following questions:

• **How old is the quilt or top?**

If the quilt or top is pre-1900, it is definitely more valuable as an antique than one made after 1940. The fabrics are older and most probably have damage from wear and exposure to light. Dyes used in 19th-century quilts are unstable, and washing may cause dyes to disappear, run or change color. Older quilts or tops are more delicate than those made in more recent times.

• **Has the quilt or top been washed?**

You can tell if a quilt has been washed. If the fabrics are still crisp and not puckered along the quilting lines, the quilt has not been washed. Washing would cause some shrinkage around the quilting stitches, and the quilt will have little ripples on the pieces between stitches. If the quilt or top has never been washed, you have a greater responsibility in making your decision.

• **Will the fabric dyes run?**

Some fabric dyes are known to run when wet. Darker fabrics with red and brown dyes are apt to bleed color onto adjacent pieces. Test every fabric individually by rubbing a white damp cloth on each one. If fabric color transfers to the cloth, the fabric will bleed when wet; do not wash.

• **Will fabric disappear when washed?**

Quilts and tops made of fabrics in which iron was used as a mordant to set the dye deteriorate with washing. When the quilt is washed, the dye will disappear along with the fabric. Dye rot is common on old quilts, especially on brown and rust fabrics. If this process has already begun, washing will make it worse and may completely destroy your quilt.

• **Does the quilt have historical value?**

If your quilt or top is very old, has never been washed and is of historical importance, do not wash. Consider how you would feel if you ruined it from washing. A quilt with exquisite quilting made before 1850 would be considered historically valuable, even without any information about its history.

• **Is the quilt or top a family heirloom?**

If your quilt or top has a known history and is an important family heirloom, consider how you would feel if you destroyed it for future generations.

If you have answered the above questions, and you still want to wash your quilt or top, you have several choices.

Spot cleaning may be all a quilt needs to look almost as good as new. Washing the entire quilt or top may be necessary for collectors who can't bear the thought of all the accumulated dust and dirt. There are those who recommend hand washing, while there are others who swear machine washing is easier on the quilt. You will have to make your own decision based on your instincts. I have tried both methods, using the washing machine with trepidation. Fortunately, I have not had any disasters.

SPOT CLEANING

Scattered spots, called foxing, are usually caused by molds. Some of these spots may look like blood, and we romanticize about the quilter bleeding as she pricked her fingers during quilting. However, the spot could be what remains of a dead bug. Humidity and temperature changes also cause this type of damage. Most of these spots can't be removed.

Spot cleaning can be done with sodium perborate which will not change the original color of the fabric. This substance is used in Clorox 2. Sodium perborate is nontoxic and biodegradable, unlike chlorine-based bleaches. It can be used to remove organic stains such as food, grass and blood. A paste made with water and other products such as Ivory Snow flakes, Shaklees Nature Bright or Biz may be used. Simply apply the paste with a brush, wait for it to dry and vacuum it away. The problem with spot cleaning is that the spot may end up being much cleaner than the rest of the quilt and show clearly when viewing.

TOTAL IMMERSION WASHING

There are several methods for total immersion washing of quilts and tops.

Hand washing in a bathtub and using your washing machine are the two most commonly recommended methods. Bathtub washing is the method of choice for conservationists who simply hate to see quilts being washed at all.

Quilt tops do not require all the steps in the bathtub method because they don't have the extra weight of batting and backing to pull on the construction stitches, and there are no quilting stitches to break. You do have to be careful of fraying seams if you wash a quilt top in the washing machine.

Cleaning Agents

The following is a list of some of the cleaning agents which may be used for washing quilts.

• Orvus is the cleaning product recommended by most textile experts. It is a cleaning product used for horses. Orvus is pH balanced and leaves no residue. It is available at animal/veterinary suppliers and at some quilt shops and museum shops. Two tablespoons is recommended for half a tub of water. Quilt Soap is a product name for Orvus especially packed with instructions for cleaning quilts by Quilter's Rule International.

• Linen Wash, made especially for cleaning fine linens, is safe for natural fibers, synthetic and blends. It works on nonorganic stains such as lipstick. The instructions on the container state that repeated use gently fades away stains. Linen Wash contains no phosphates, bleach or caustics, has a neutral pH and is biodegradable.

• Ensure Quilt Wash from Mountain Mist is specially formulated for cleaning quilts and other needlework.

Instructions for both hand and machine washing are included on the container. Ensure contains nonionic and anionic surfactants and triethanolamine which helps it to attract different types of soil molecules.

• Victorian Soak is a powdered product used to remove stains and age spots and to brighten textiles made using natural fibers. It contains sodium percarbonate.

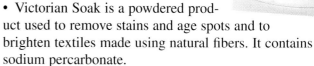

• Lard and Lye Soap is advertised as the Appalachian tradition for cleaning clothes and quilting fabrics. It is made with a time-tested recipe made with lard and lye. It is all-natural and can clean and whiten without damage to fragile threads.

• Quiltwash from Craftgard is a specially formulated washing product for quilts.

- Natural homemade buttermilk wash can be used but is expensive. For every gallon of water, add one quart of buttermilk with 1-percent or less butterfat content and one tablespoon of lemon juice.

- Biz and Ivory Snow Flakes are commercial laundry products that are easily found at most supermarkets. Biz is known for its whitening ability, while Ivory is famous for being gentle.

Washing in a Bathtub

If you choose to immerse your quilt in water for washing, some experts recommend special treatment. The main concern after color migration is damage to fibers caused by the weight of the water. This can be somewhat controlled by taking precautions to avoid squeezing and lifting water-soaked quilts. The following is a short step-by-step list of directions for washing your quilt in the bathtub:

Step 1. Fill a clean bathtub with lukewarm water.

Step 2. Add the chosen cleaning agent, if you have decided one is necessary, referring to the product instructions for ratio of soap to water.

Step 3. Place a large white sheet over the sides of the bathtub. The sheet will act as a sling to lift the wet quilt out of the tub later.

Step 4. Fold the quilt in layers similar to a fan. Lay the folded quilt on top of the sheet.

Step 5. Let the quilt soak in the water for up to 12 hours, changing the water several times, until the water remains clear.

Step 6. If a cleaning agent was added, it must be totally removed from the quilt. Change the water until there is no evidence of suds. Do not wring or rub the quilt during this process. Some conservationists recommend using distilled water during the final rinse. City dwellers probably have chlorine added to their water to make it safe for drinking, while country dwellers commonly use well water which either contains some naturally occuring minerals or salt from a water conditioner.

Step 7. Leave the quilt in the bathtub for several hours to let water drain from the quilt. Squeezing or wringing could break quilting threads or damage fabrics.

Step 8. Prepare a surface outside in a shaded area, not under a tree or in the direct sunlight, on which to lay the quilt flat. Large, light-colored absorbent cotton towels or a thick, quilted cotton mattress pad make perfect absorbent surfaces.

Step 9. Lift the quilt out of the water inside the sheet with assistance from a helper, if possible.

Step 10. Move the quilt to the prepared surface and spread flat, making sure corners are square, and cover with more towels. Press on towels to help remove excess water. Remove these towels and cover with a sheet.

Step 11. Let the quilt dry all day. If not fully dry, lay out on a covered surface inside to be sure it is completely dry before storing.

Washing in a Washing Machine

Should you choose to wash your quilt in the washing machine, you will find that you use less water, causing less strain on the fibers, and it is simply easier.

Step 1. Set the machine on the gentle or lingerie cycle.

Step 2. Fill the washer with lukewarm water, adding cleaning agent if desired.

Step 3. Move the quilt around using your hands; let soak.

Step 4. Move the machine's knob to the rinse cycle to remove excess water.

Step 5. Remove quilt from washer and dry thoroughly as for hand washing.

STORING

Storage of antique quilts can be a problem if you have many quilts and not much space.

Most conservationists recommend special storage containers and refolding to reduce stress on folds. Most agree that acid-free storage containers are the best choice while plastic is the absolute worst choice. If you have valuable quilts to store, consider the following options:

- Acid-free, lignin and sulphur-free boxes. Physical contact with acidic substances causes fabric deterioration and staining. This type of box protects the quilt from light and dust. Quilts are folded with acid-free paper scrunched into folds to prevent crisp folds that can break fibers. Refold quilts periodically to move folds to different areas.

• Rolling tubes. Rolling quilts on acid-free tubes decreases fabric breaks resulting from folds. You may choose brown kraft tubes covered with Tyvek or archival-quality polyester film or a chemically inert polyethylene plastic tube. Roll the quilt with the design side out; wrap the out-side layers with Tyvek (chemically inert, water-resistant, fabric-like material) or acid-free tissue paper. Store on a shelf or under a bed, with ends of tube supported to keep weight off quilt and keeping areas dust free.

• Choose a room with constant temperature and stable humidity. Attics (too hot) and basements (too humid) are not suitable storage areas. Cedar chests are not good choices because of the wood and cedar oils, unless lined with Tyvek. Do not use sachets or deodorizers or moth balls with your quilts. Photographs and other items should not be stored with quilts.

DISPLAYING QUILTS

I believe quilts should be enjoyed, not always just wrapped and stored away where no one can see them. Using your antique quilts does require some special precautions to reduce further damage. Natural aging is expected; humans don't look the same when they are 70 as they did when they were 5, so why should a quilt?

Choices for display include hanging on a rack, along a railing, on a wall or on beds. These display methods do require some special tricks to avoid abnormal damage.

• Keep pets away from antique quilts. Cats and dogs can cause extreme damage from hair, dirt and tears caused by claws. If you have pets be sure your quilts are protected from them.

• Display quilts on a spare bed, rotating them frequently. If you have a spare bed, layering many quilts on top of the bed is a great storage choice while allowing them to be seen.

• When folding a quilt over a wooden rack or stair railing, place a cotton pillowcase or piece of doubled muslin between the quilt and the wood layers. Do not drape quilts over tables or chairs or other objects that may have sharp corner edges.

• Refold folded quilts often to reduce stress on folds.

• Add a hanging sleeve on the back top edge of a quilt for hanging; do not use pins, tacks or push pins to hold in place. Hanging sleeves over rods distributes the weight evenly across the top of the quilt and reduces stress on the fibers and stitches.

• Use hook-and-loop tape such as Velcro to attach quilt to a frame. The hook part of the tape should be stitched to cotton twill tape. The twill tape should be hand-stitched to the quilt's edges.

• Avoid displaying quilts in areas where sunlight could shine directly on them. Both sunlight and artificial light can cause fading.

• Rotate hanging quilts every six months. Air out and vacuum displayed quilts before storing.

RESOURCES

If you are more interested in proper conservation and storage of your antique or vintage quilts, you have help available in many forms. Begin at your local library. There are many great books, both old and new, available with good information. As previously stated, these sources do not all agree about these subjects, but the more you learn, the better informed decision you can make for yourself.

Search online choices. This could take days. Even if you don't own a computer or have online access, your local library should have. Whether you are computer savvy or a novice, it is easy to get information. Don't be afraid to ask for help.

When I was searching for information, I simply opened my Netscape home page and typed in "quilt care" in the search box. The number of options available was listed in the thousands. I visited many Web sites and have listed a few of them here to get you started. Many of these have links to other related sites. Quilt preservation products can be purchased through many of these sites. If you can't find products such as acid-free boxes locally, you can order them online.

Institutions

Smithsonian Information Center
P.O. Box 37012
SI Building, Room 153, MRC 010
Washington, DC 20013-7012
www.si.edu/visit/InfoCenter/start.htm

American Textile History Museum
491 Dutton St.
Lowell, MA 01854-4221
(978) 441-0400
www.athm.org

Textile Conservation Workshop
Main Street
South Salem, NY 10590
(914) 763-5805
www.rap-arcc.org/welcome/tcw.htm

Books

First Aid for Family Quilts by Nancy O'Bryant Puentes

Quilt Restoration: A Practical Guide by Camille Dalphond Cognac

Clean It Fast, Clean It Right from art experts at the Guggenheim Museum

The Care and Preservation of Textiles by Karen Finch and Greta Putnam

Online Sites

www.quilthistory.com

www.rmqm.org/preservi.htm

www.kirkcollection.com

www.quilting.about.com/msubhist.htm

1 Close inspection shows a section of the print in this patch is missing. The dye made for this section is responsible for this damage.

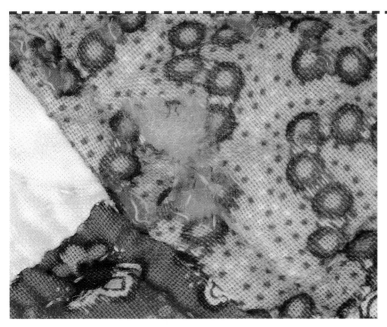

2 The *Shadow Star Antique Quilt* demonstrates the effects of overexposure to light. Where the green fabric was exposed to the light (left), the color has faded considerably from the original dark green (right).

3

Little brown age spots have accumulated over the years.

4

It is apparent that this quilt has been washed as the quilt stitches pull the fabric and batting into little wrinkles.

5

This quilt has never been washed and the pencil marks for quilting still show. The fabrics are still crisp and flat.

These blocks show signs of being stored in a moist, humid place. These water-stain lines cannot be removed.

Some sort of stain, whether from an insect or moisture, caused a hole to rot in this pieced block.

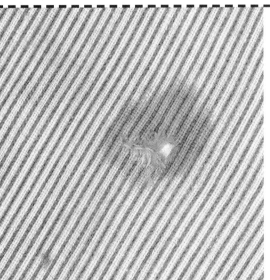

The dyes used in these old patches caused the fabrics to deteriorate.

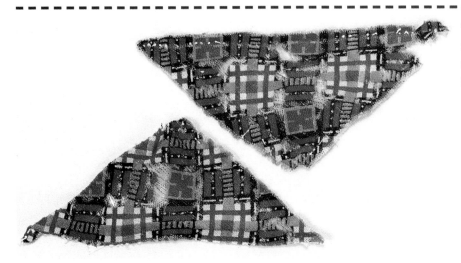

Sunflower Antique Quilt

The Sunflower pattern was printed in Needlecraft Magazine *in 1931.*
The antique quilt shown must have been made in that same time period.

PROJECT NOTES

The Sunflower pattern is not simple; it can be machine-pieced and appliquéd, or simply appliquéd using fusible products. The quilt shown was hand-pieced, hand-appliquéd and hand-quilted. The stitches in all techniques are tiny and even. The quilter was a master. Her work is wonderful. The only criticism I can make is that the blue marking dots show on some of the fabric pieces, and the pencil lines used to mark the quilting are still visible, although not terribly obvious.

The fabric color choices baffle me. I am not sure why the dark yellow print was used in the alternating blocks while the appliqué pieces are all solids. The dark peach solid does not match the yellow print. I would never make these fabric choices, but altogether, it works. I would love to see this with the dark yellow print and the yellow solid in the appliquéd blocks.

If you choose to try machine methods, the pieces can be overlapped and fused in place on the background. Cut your pieces with a slight overlap using the template without seam allowance, adding 1/8" to the inside curved edge. Begin with a 3" circle in the center, placing pieces around the circle, overlapping the inside edges as shown in Figure 1; do not fuse in place until all pieces have been placed and the arrangement is perfect.

Figure 1
Place pieces around a 3" circle, overlapping the inside edges.

The instructions given are for the quilt as it was originally made. The dark yellow print used in the alternating squares suggests a late-1800s time period, but the pattern appeared in 1931. The yellow and peach solids reflect that time period. Maybe this quilter was like many of us today and had a stash of fabric saved for her perfect quilt. We will never know, will we?

PROJECT SPECIFICATIONS

Quilt Size: 86" x 99"

Block Size: 13" x 13"

Number of Blocks: 21

MATERIALS

- 2 yards pale yellow solid
- 2 3/4 yards muslin
- 3 1/2 yards dark peach solid
- 3 1/2 yards dark yellow print
- Backing 90" x 103"
- Batting 90" x 103"
- All-purpose thread to match fabrics
- Yellow and cream hand-quilting thread
- Heat-resistant template material
- Basic sewing supplies and tools, rotary cutter, mat and ruler and water-erasable marker or pencil

Sunflower
13" x 13" Block

INSTRUCTIONS

Step 1. Prepare templates using pattern pieces given. A is the template including seam allowance and B is the template without seam allowance. Cut A pieces as directed on the piece for one block; repeat for 21 blocks. Using the B piece, mark the seam lines on the wrong side of each piece using a water-erasable marker or pencil.

Step 2. Cut 21 squares muslin 13 1/2" x 13 1/2"; fold and crease each square to find the center.

Step 3. Cut 21 squares dark yellow print 13 1/2" x 13 1/2" for alternating squares; set aside.

Step 4. To complete one block, sew a pale yellow solid A to a dark peach solid A beginning at the narrow ends and stitching only on the marked seam line as shown in Figure 2; continue stitching in units of two A pieces each.

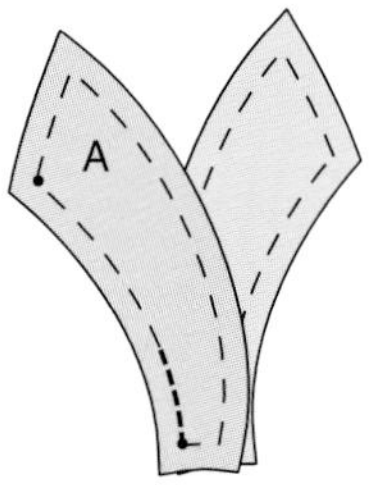

Step 5. Join two pieced units to make six four-unit sections. Join these sections to make halves; join the halves to complete the circle shape. Press with seams in one direction.

Figure 2
Sew a pale yellow solid A to a dark peach solid A beginning at the narrow ends and stitching only on the marked seam line.

Step 6. Insert the heat-resistant B template between stitched A pieces on the wrong side of the pieced unit as

shown in Figure 3; press seam allowance over B on both inside and outside edges as shown in Figure 4.

Figure 3
Insert the heat-resistant B template between stitched A pieces on the wrong side of the pieced unit.

Figure 4
Press seam allowance over B on both inside and outside edges.

Step 7. Trace the 3" circle shape on the center of a creased muslin square using the water-erasable marker or pencil as shown in Figure 5.

Figure 5
Trace the 3" circle shape on the center of a creased muslin square.

Step 8. Place the pieced A unit on the muslin square, aligning pressed center edges with the drawn circle shape; hand-appliqué center in place.

Step 9. Baste outside edges of the A unit to the muslin square; hand-appliqué in place. Remove basting when stitching is complete. Repeat for 21 blocks.

Step 10. Join three appliquéd blocks with three alternating squares to make a row as shown in Figure 6; press seams in one direction. Repeat for seven rows.

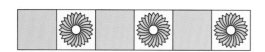

Figure 6
Join 3 appliquéd blocks with 3 alternating squares to make a row.

Step 11. Join the rows referring to the Placement Diagram for positioning; press seams in one direction.

Step 12. Cut and piece two strips dark peach solid each 4 1/2" x 89" and 4 1/2" x 102". Center and sew the shorter strips to the top and bottom, and longer strips to opposite long sides, mitering corners. Trim excess at miter; press mitered seams open and border seams toward strips.

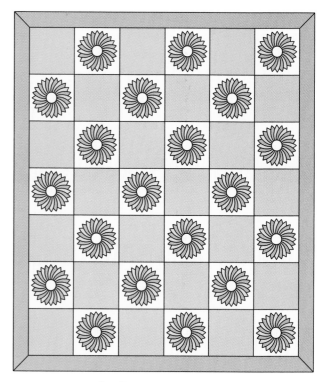

Sunflower Antique Quilt
Placement Diagram
86" x 99"

Step 13. Sandwich batting between the completed top and prepared backing piece; pin or baste layers together to hold flat.

Step 14. Quilt as desired by hand or machine. *Note: The quilt shown was hand-quilted 1/4" inside A pieces using yellow hand-quilting thread and in a 3/4" diagonal grid in the background and border strips using cream hand-quilting thread. The alternating blocks were quilted in a diagonal diamond grid using cream hand-quilting thread.*

Step 15. Cut ten 2 1/4" by fabric width strips dark yellow print. Join the strips on short ends to make one long strip for binding.

Step 16. Fold binding strip with wrong sides together along length and press. Pin to the quilt top edges with raw edges even. Stitch all around, mitering corners and overlapping ends. Turn binding to the backside; hand-stitch in place to finish. ❖

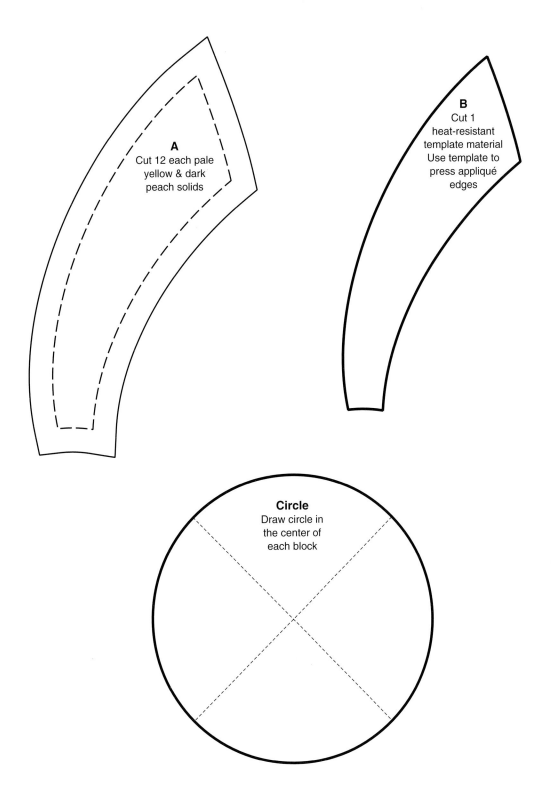

A
Cut 12 each pale
yellow & dark
peach solids

B
Cut 1
heat-resistant
template material
Use template to
press appliqué
edges

Circle
Draw circle in
the center of
each block

Sunflower
Magazine Holder

One block is useful in this magazine or sewing tool holder
which can be used on the side of a bed or over the arm of a chair.

PROJECT NOTES

I could sew from an early age and made a crazy quilt when I was 10. I made Barbie® clothes at a younger age and many of my own clothes in my teen years. As a 4-H member and the oldest of six girls, sewing was a natural. I became a home economics major in college, and later I taught this subject in middle school. Why is this important? I still had to take a beginning quiltmaking class. Quilting is not exactly like any other kind of sewing. It helps to have good sewing skills because it is easier to become a more exact quilter, but there are many differences between sewing and quilting.

The class project was a Dresden Plate pillow. The Dresden Plate is the perfect project for learning hand methods. You learn to make templates, mark seam lines, hand-piece, center on a background and hand-appliqué perfect curves in place. The second phase includes sandwiching the batting and backing, and hand-quilting a design on the finished pillow top. Then the sewing skills take over to complete the pillow.

The reason that is relevant here is that the Sunflower pattern is very similar to the Dresden Plate design. It includes all of the same skills. I have not made another Dresden Plate since that first one, and making this block brought back a lot of memories of that experience. I am pleased that I had not forgotten these skills since most of my quilted projects are machine-pieced and -appliquéd— my hand-piecing days are few and far between.

I do remember that my Dresden Plate circle did not lie flat on the background the first time around. I had to adjust many of the seams. This Sunflower design was perfect without any adjustments. I was thrilled!

I am disappointed that I did not use the darker yellow print in my blocks with the yellow solid. I tried to match the antique quilt, but could not find the exact dark peach or the same yellow solid. I was able to find the perfect dark yellow print reproduction fabric. I really wished I had used it in the A pieces with the yellow solid. I did not wish to make a second block, however, so I finished the project with my first block.

PROJECT SPECIFICATIONS

Project Size: 14 1/2" x 30"

Block Size: 13" x 13"

Number of Blocks: 1

MATERIALS

- 1/4 yard pale yellow solid
- 1/4 yard light yellow print
- 1/2 yard cream-on-cream print
- 1 yard dark yellow print
- Backing 18" x 34"
- Batting 16" x 16" and 18" x 34"
- All-purpose thread to match fabrics
- Yellow and cream machine-quilting thread
- Heat-resistant template material
- Basic sewing supplies and tools, rotary cutter, mat and ruler and water-erasable marker or pencil

Sunflower
13" x 13" Block

INSTRUCTIONS

Making the Block

Step 1. Prepare templates using pattern pieces given. A is the template including seam allowance and B is the template without seam allowance. Cut A pieces as directed on the piece. Using the B piece, mark the seam lines on the wrong side of each piece using a water-erasable marker or pencil.

Step 2. Cut one square cream-on-cream print 13 1/2" x 13 1/2"; fold and crease to find the center.

Step 3. To complete the block, sew a pale yellow solid A to a light yellow print A beginning at the narrow ends and stitching only on the marked seam line as shown in Figure 1; continue stitching in units of two A pieces each.

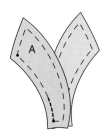

Figure 1
Sew a pale yellow solid A to a light yellow print A beginning at the narrow ends and stitching only on the marked seam line.

Step 4. Join two pieced units to make six four-unit sections. Join these sections to make halves; join the halves to complete the circle shape. Press with seams in one direction.

Step 5. Insert the heat-resistant B template between stitched A pieces on the wrong side of the pieced unit as shown in Figure 2; press seam allowance over B on both inside and outside edges as shown in Figure 3.

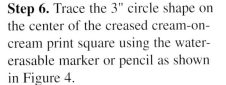

Figure 2
Insert the heat-resistant B template between stitched A pieces on the wrong side of the pieced unit.

Figure 3
Press seam allowance over B on both inside and outside edges.

Step 6. Trace the 3" circle shape on the center of the creased cream-on-cream print square using the water-erasable marker or pencil as shown in Figure 4.

Figure 4
Trace the 3" circle shape on the center of the creased cream-on-cream print square.

Step 7. Place the pieced A unit on the cream-on-cream print square, aligning pressed center edges with the drawn circle shape; hand-appliqué center in place.

Step 8. Baste outside edges of the A unit to the muslin square; hand-appliqué in place. Remove basting when stitching is complete.

Step 9. Cut two 1 1/2" by fabric width strips dark yellow print; fold with wrong sides together along length and press. Cut into two 13 1/2" and two 15" lengths.

Step 10. Cut two strips each 1 1/4" x 13 1/2" and 1 1/4" x 15" pale yellow solid.

Step 11. Pin the folded 13 1/2" strips with raw edges even on two opposite sides of the appliquéd block; machine-baste in place as shown in Figure 5.

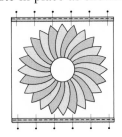

Figure 5
Pin the folded 13 1/2" strips with raw edges even on opposite sides of the appliquéd block; machine-baste in place

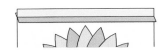

Figure 6
Press seams toward the pale yellow solid strips, leaving the folded strip flat.

Step 12. Pin the 1 1/4" x 13 1/2" strips pale yellow solid right sides together with the basted strips; stitch. Press seams toward the pale yellow solid strips, leaving the

folded strip flat as shown in Figure 6. Repeat with remaining folded strips and pale yellow solid strips on the remaining sides.

Step 13. Cut one 16" x 16" square cream-on-cream print for backing. Sandwich the batting square between the completed block top and the backing square; pin or baste layers together to hold flat.

Step 14. Machine-quilt in the ditch of seams in the pieced sections of the block, around outer edge and 1/4" echo lines using cream machine-quilting thread. Machine-quilt in the ditch of seams on border strips using yellow machine-quilting thread. When quilting is complete, remove pins or basting; trim batting and backing even with the quilted block. Set aside.

EXTENSION PANEL

Step 1. Cut one 16" x 32" rectangle dark yellow print.

Step 2. Mark a 2" diagonal crosshatch grid on the rectangle using the water-erasable marker or pencil.

Step 3. Sandwich the 18" x 34" batting between the dark yellow print rectangle and the 18" x 34" backing piece.

Step 4. Machine-quilt on marked lines using yellow machine-quilting thread.

Step 5. When quilting is complete, trim quilted rectangle to 15" x 30 1/2".

FINISHING

Step 1. Cut three 2 1/4" by fabric width strips dark yellow print. Join strips on short ends to make one long strip for binding.

Step 2. Fold the binding strip with wrong sides together along length and press.

Step 3. Cut one 16" length of binding. Pin the strip to one edge of the quilted block with raw edges even; stitch. Turn binding to the backside and hand- or machine-stitch in place.

Step 4. Pin the quilted block with wrong side against the dark yellow print side of the quilted rectangle and raw edges even as shown in Figure 7; machine-baste around the three sides to hold, again referring to Figure 7.

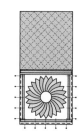

Figure 7
Pin the quilted block with wrong side against the dark yellow print side of the quilted rectangle and raw edges even; machine-baste to hold.

Step 5. Pin remaining prepared binding to outside edges of the completed top and stitch, overlapping at beginning and end. Turn binding to the backside and hand- or

Sunflower Magazine Holder
Placement Diagram
14 1/2" x 30"

machine-stitch in place to finish.

Step 6. Place extension end of magazine holder between box spring and mattress or over arm of stuffed chair. The block pocket will remain exposed for use. ❖

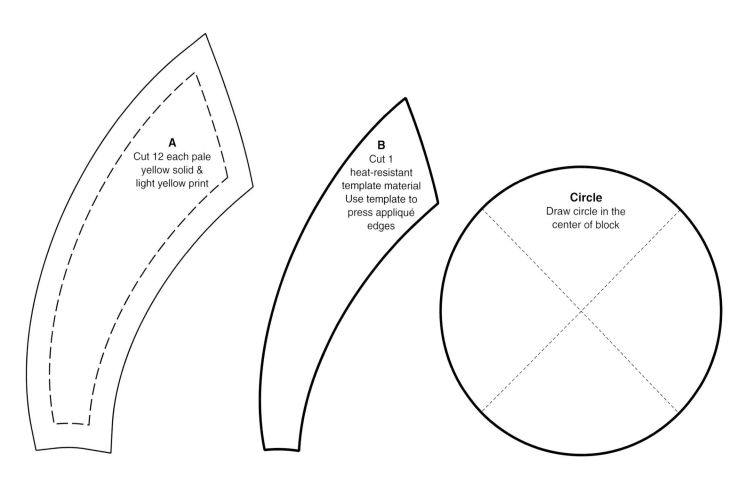

A
Cut 12 each pale yellow solid & light yellow print

B
Cut 1 heat-resistant template material Use template to press appliqué edges

Circle
Draw circle in the center of block

Blossoming Tulips Antique Quilt

Pretty tulip appliqué in pink is typical of the 1930s. This quilt has a never-used look which means it was probably stored in a trunk to be used only for company.

PROJECT NOTES

Several of my antique quilts still have visible pencil marks. This quilt is one of them. It has never been washed, so the marks are really dark (they do take away from the beauty of the quilt up close). However, I hate to wash it because it appears that it was never used. The fabrics are crisp and just like new.

This is a dilemma; wash to get out the marks and make a more attractive quilt or leave as is in the original condition. For now I have chosen to leave it as it is. One day, should I decide I would like to use this pretty quilt on a bed and find the pencil marks bother me, I might decide to wash it (refer to Caring for Vintage Quilts on page 47).

The tulips were hand-appliquéd on background blocks which were set together in an unusual arrangement as can be seen in the photo of the quilt and in the Placement Diagram. The stitching is well-done. The hand-quilting stitches are small and even, but are lost in the pencil marks.

PROJECT SPECIFICATIONS

Quilt Size: 80" x 80"

Block Size: 12" x 12"

Number of Blocks: 36

MATERIALS

- 1/2 yard pink print
- 5/8 yard medium green solid
- 5/8 yard dark green solid
- 2 yards pink solid
- 4 1/4 yards muslin
- Backing 84" x 84"
- Batting 84" x 84"
- All-purpose thread to match fabrics
- White hand-quilting thread
- 3/8"-wide bias bar
- Basic sewing supplies and tools, rotary cutter, mat and ruler

Blossoming Tulip
12" x 12" Block

INSTRUCTIONS

Step 1. Prepare templates for tulip and leaf shapes using patterns given; cut as directed on each piece for one block, adding a 1/8"–1/4" seam allowance to each piece when cutting. Repeat for 36 blocks.

Step 2. Cut 36 squares muslin 12 1/2" x 12 1/2"; fold and crease each square to find the center.

Step 3. Cut 1 1/4"-wide strips dark green solid on the diagonal to make bias strips. Join the strips on the short ends to make 17 yards bias.

Step 4. Fold the bias with wrong sides together along length; stitch a 1/8" seam. Cut the bias into 36 pieces 6 3/4" long and 72 pieces 5" long.

Figure 1
Insert the bias bar in each cut strip, centering seam.

Step 5. Insert the bias bar in each cut strip, centering seam as shown in Figure 1; press.

Step 6. To complete one block, center three tulip motifs, two leaves and three stems in numerical order on one muslin square referring to Figure 2; pin or baste pieces in place.

Figure 2
Center 3 tulip motifs, 2 leaves and 3 stems in numerical order on 1 muslin square.

Step 7. Using thread to match fabrics, hand-appliqué shapes in place in numerical order. Repeat for 36 blocks.

Step 8. Join six blocks to make an A row as shown in Figure 3; repeat for three A rows. Press seams in one direction.

Figure 3
Join 6 blocks to make an A row.

Step 9. Join six blocks to make a B row as shown in Figure 4; repeat for three B rows. Press seams in one direction.

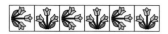

Figure 4
Join 6 blocks to make a B row.

Leaf
Cut 2 medium green solid
(reverse 1)

Tulip Center
Cut 3 pink print

Tulip Petals
Cut 3 each
pink solid

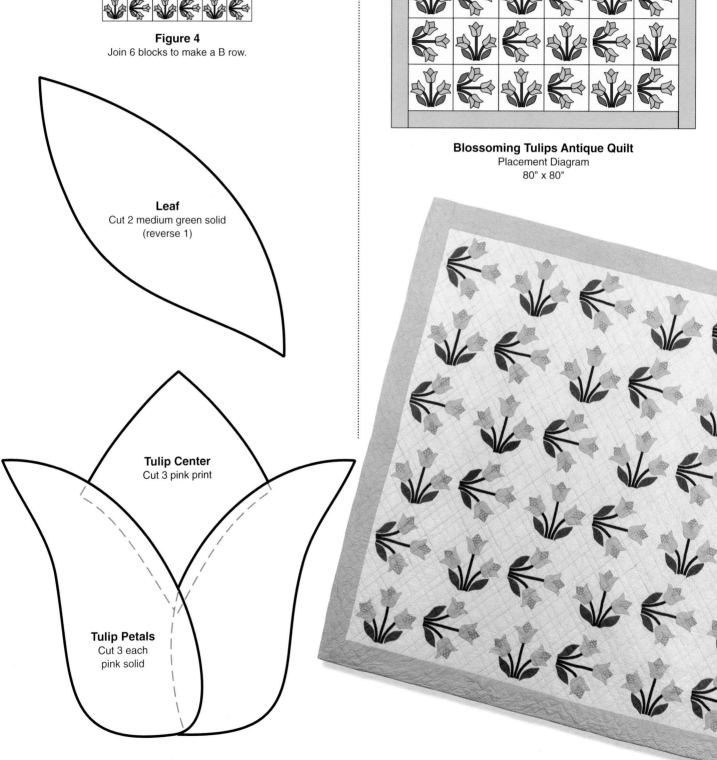

Blossoming Tulips Antique Quilt
Placement Diagram
80" x 80"

4" x 72"

4" x 80"

Step 10. Join the rows, beginning with the A row and alternating A and B rows; press seams in one direction.

Step 11. Cut and piece two strips pink solid each 4 1/2" x 72 1/2" and 4 1/2" x 80 1/2". Sew the shorter strips to the top and bottom and longer strips to opposite sides; press seams toward strips.

Step 12. Sandwich batting between the completed top and prepared backing piece; pin or baste layers together to hold flat.

Step 13. Quilt as desired by hand or machine, stopping quilting 1" from quilt edges. ***Note:*** *The quilt shown was hand-quilted in a diagonal grid using white hand-quilting thread.*

Step 14. Trim batting 1/4" smaller than quilt top all around. Trim backing even with quilt top edge.

Step 15. Turn quilt top and backing edges 1/4" to the wrong side; press. Hand-stitch the layers together to finish. ❖

Tulip Pillowcases

Make some pillowcases to match your Blossoming Tulips *quilt and your decorating is complete.*

PROJECT NOTES

Matching pillowcases make any quilt a hit. Quilts are not intended to tuck under pillows as are bedspreads, so pillow shams or matching pillowcases add the perfect touch.

These pillowcases were made using reproduction 1930s prints. They are not the exact fabrics used in the original antique quilt, but the colors and design work well. The tulip motif was reduced to make it fit a pillowcase band.

PROJECT SPECIFICATIONS

Pillowcase Size: 31" x 20"

MATERIALS

- 6" x 10" rectangle pink solid
- 1/4 yard green solid
- 1 yard muslin
- 1 1/2 yards pink print
- Pink and green all-purpose thread
- 1/4 yard fusible transfer web
- 3/8 yard fabric stabilizer
- Basic sewing supplies and tools, rotary cutter, mat and ruler

INSTRUCTIONS

Step 1. Prepare templates for tulip and leaf shapes using patterns given.

Step 2. Trace shapes onto the paper side of the fusible transfer web as directed on the patterns for number to cut. Cut out shapes leaving a margin around each one.

Step 3. Fuse shapes to the wrong side of fabrics as directed on each piece for color; cut out shapes on traced lines. Remove paper backing.

Step 4. Cut two 5 1/2" x 40 3/4" strips muslin for appliqué strips; fold each strip to make a double layer 5 1/2" wide.

Step 5. Arrange three tulip motifs with leaves on each strip with tulip center shape under petal shape, leaving 1 1/2" at folded edge, 1" between motifs and 1 7/8" at the open edge as shown in Figure 1; fuse shapes in place and unfold strips.

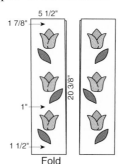

Figure 1
Arrange 3 motifs on the muslin strips.

Step 6. Cut two 5 1/2" x 20" pieces fabric stabilizer; pin one piece under each fused section of each muslin strip. Machine satin-stitch around each shape and on marked detail lines using all-purpose thread to match fabrics.

Step 7. Cut four 1 1/2" x 40 3/4" strips green solid. Sew a strip to opposite long sides of each appliquéd muslin strip; press seams toward green solid strips.

Step 8. Cut two 3 1/2" x 40 3/4" strips pink print; sew a strip to each green solid strip to complete the appliquéd bands referring to Figure 2. *Note: Remember that you need a right and left pillowcase.*

Figure 2
Sew the pink print strip to the green solid strip to complete the appliquéd band.

Step 9. Cut two 21 5/8" x 40 3/4" rectangles pink print. Sew a rectangle to each appliquéd band on the green solid strip sides; press seams toward green solid strips.

Step 10. Cut two 10 3/4" x 40 3/4" rectangles muslin for appliquéd-band lining Sew a rectangle to the appliquéd-band end of each stitched unit; press seams toward muslin strips and topstitch as shown in Figure 3.

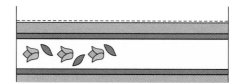

Figure 3
Press lining and pieced section with seam toward lining piece and topstitch as shown.

Step 11. Fold stitched piece with wrong sides together and raw edges even; stitch a 1/8" seam along side and bottom edge. Turn wrong side out; press seam flat.

Step 12. Stitch along the pressed-and-stitched edge with a 1/4" seam allowance to enclose previously stitched seam as shown in Figure 4. **Note:** *This*

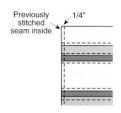

Figure 4
Stitch along the pressed-and-stitched edge with a 1/4" seam allowance to enclose previously stitched seam.

seam is called a French seam. It is a sturdy seam as there are no raw edges to wear.

Step 13. Fold under 1/2" along the muslin strip edge; press. Fold the lining section to the inside to cover seam between appliquéd band and the pink print section; baste in place, carefully lining up edges as shown in Figure 5.

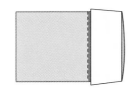

Figure 5
Fold the lining section to the inside to cover seam between the appliquéd band and pink print section; press.

Step 14. From the right side, topstitch close to seam to catch basted section. Topstitch in the ditch between muslin and green solid strips to finish. Repeat for second pillowcase. ❖

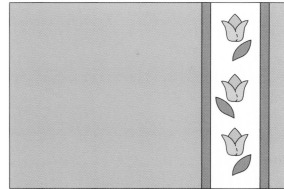

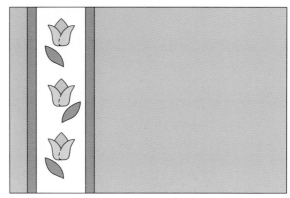

Tulip Pillowcases
Placement Diagram
31" x 20"

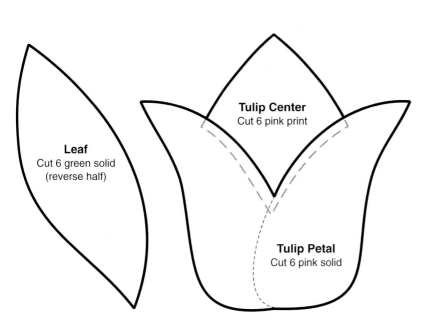

Leaf
Cut 6 green solid
(reverse half)

Tulip Center
Cut 6 pink print

Tulip Petal
Cut 6 pink solid

Evening Star Antique Quilt

Tattered quilts can be used as decorative accents. This green, red and white star quilt makes the perfect tree skirt for your holiday.

PROJECT NOTES

The red and green prints in this quilt appear to be from the late 1800s. The pattern is identified as Evening Star in *The Encyclopedia of Pieced Patterns* by Barbara Brackman, with the origin credited to the Ladies Art Co., dating from 1895 and before. The green print has tiny yellow dots and black lines, and the red print has white dots and black lines around white shapes. The white on some blocks has popped out. The whole quilt is quite faded with one side being more faded than the other. The binding is tattered. In spite of the damage, the quilt is soft and still has plenty of life left in it, if it is treated carefully.

I have used this quilt around the base of one of my Christmas trees. Because I have several decorated trees with only a few gifts under each of them, the quilt beneath can still be seen and appreciated.

The Evening Star pattern is easy to make using quick-cutting and -piecing methods, although the original quilt-maker undoubtedly used templates. It was hand-pieced and heavily hand-quilted even though there is no batting between the layers.

PROJECT SPECIFICATIONS

Quilt Size: 79 5/8" x 91"

Block Size: 8" x 8"

Number of Blocks: 56

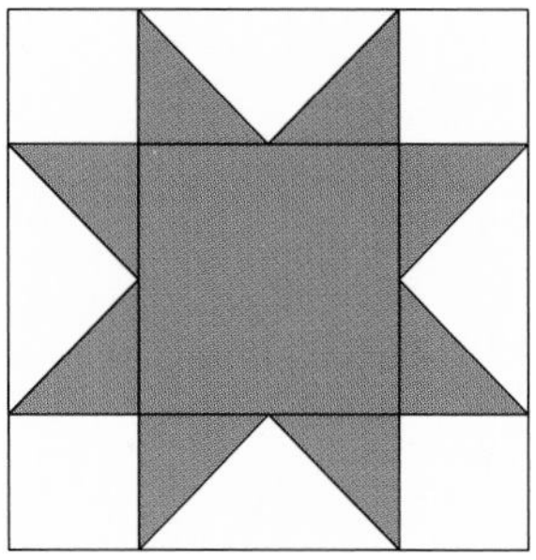

MATERIALS

- 5/8 yard pink print for binding
- 3 yards muslin
- 3 1/4 yards red print
- 4 yards green print
- Backing 84" x 95"
- Batting 84" x 95"
- All-purpose thread to match fabrics
- White hand-quilting thread
- Basic sewing tools and supplies, rotary cutter, mat and ruler, and water-erasable marker or pencil

Evening Star
8" x 8" Block

INSTRUCTIONS

Step 1. Cut seven strips red print 4 1/2" by fabric width; subcut each strip into 4 1/2" square segments for A. You will need 56 A squares.

Step 2. Cut 28 strips red print 2 1/2" by fabric width; subcut each strip into 2 1/2" square segments for B. You will need 448 B squares. Draw a diagonal line from corner to corner on the wrong side of each B square.

Step 3. Cut 14 strips muslin 4 1/2" by fabric width; subcut into 2 1/2" segments for C. You will need 224 C rectangles.

Step 4. Cut 14 strips muslin 2 1/2" by fabric width; subcut into 2 1/2" segments for D. You will need 224 D squares.

Step 5. Place a B square right sides together with C as shown in Figure 1; stitch on the marked line. Trim away excess to make a 1/4" seam allowance as shown in Figure 2; press B to the right side.

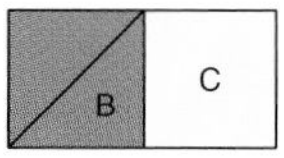

Figure 1
Place a B square right sides together with C.

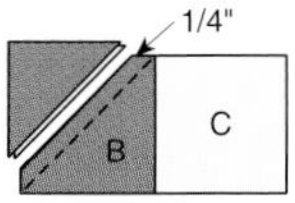

Figure 2
Trim away excess to make a 1/4" seam allowance.

Step 6. Place a second B square on the remaining end of C and stitch as in Step 5. Press and trim off triangle points to complete one B-C unit as shown in Figure 3. Repeat for 224 B-C units.

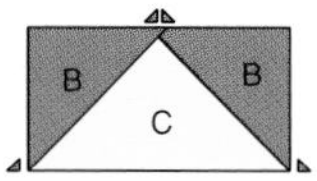

Figure 3
Trim off triangle points to complete 1 B-C unit.

Figure 4
Sew a B-C unit to opposite sides of A.

Figure 5
Sew a D square to the ends of 2 B-C units.

Step 7. To piece one block, sew a B-C unit to opposite sides of A as shown in Figure 4; press seams toward A.

Step 8. Sew a D square to the ends of two B-C units as shown in Figure 5; repeat. Sew a B-C-D unit to the sides of the A-B-C unit to complete one block as shown in Figure 6; press seams toward A. Repeat for 56 blocks.

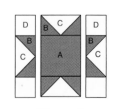

Figure 6
Sew a B-C-D unit to the sides of the A-B-C unit to complete 1 block.

Step 9. Cut 11 strips green print 8 1/2" by fabric width; subcut into

8 1/2" squares for E. You will need 42 E squares.

Step 10. Cut seven squares green print 12 5/8" x 12 5/8". Cut each square on both diagonals as shown in Figure 7 to make F triangles. You will need 26 F triangles; set aside two triangles for another project.

Step 11. Cut two squares red print 6 5/8" x 6 5/8". Cut each square in half on one diagonal to make G triangles; you will need four G triangles.

Step 12. Arrange the pieced blocks with the E squares and F triangles to make diagonal rows referring to Figure 8. Join blocks in diagonal rows; press seams in adjacent rows in opposite directions. Join the rows and add G to the corners to complete the pieced top.

Figure 7
Cut each 12 5/8" square on both diagonals to make F triangles.

Evening Star Antique Quilt
Placement Diagram
79 5/8" x 91"

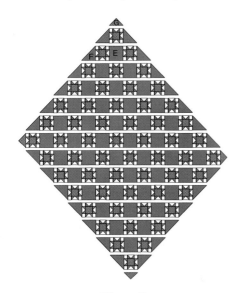

Figure 8
Arrange the pieced blocks with the E squares and F triangles to make diagonal rows: add G to corners.

Step 13. Mark a chosen quilting design on the top using a water-erasable marker or pencil. **Note:** *The quilt shown was hand-quilted using white hand-quilting thread in a 3/4" diagonal grid on the E squares and a 3/4" grid following*

the triangle shapes of F and G. The A pieces were quilted though all centers, the D squares with an X through the center and the C triangles with a line through the center as well as in the ditch of all seams.

Step 14. Sandwich batting between the completed top and prepared backing piece; pin or baste layers together to hold.

Step 15. Quilt on marked lines or as desired. When quilting is complete, trim edges even; remove pins or basting.

Step 16. Cut nine strips pink print 2 1/4" by fabric width. Join strips on short ends to make one long strip for binding.

Step 17. Fold binding strip with wrong sides together along length and press. Pin to the quilt top edges with raw edges even. Stitch all around, mitering corners and overlapping ends. Turn binding to the backside; hand-stitch in place to finish. ❖

Evening Star Gift Bag

Gift bags not only are functional, they add a decorative accent under the tree.
This gift bag coordinates with an antique quilt used as a tree skirt.

PROJECT NOTES

The fabrics used to create the gift bag shown are almost the exact same fabrics used in the *Evening Star* antique quilt, except 100 years newer! The green fabric, although faded in the antique quilt, is nearly an exact copy of the original fabric. The yellow dots and black lines are almost gone on the antique fabric, but when it was new, it looked much like the reproduction print. The red print also has white flowers framed in black, similar to that used in the bag.

Imagine the antique quilt when it was new with the colors of the gift bag. A quilt made using this pattern and these fabrics would be easy to reproduce and would be beautiful on a bed or under a tree with several coordinating gift bags.

PROJECT SPECIFICATIONS

Bag Size: 16" x 22"

Block Size: 8" x 8"

Number of Blocks: 1

MATERIALS

- 1/2 yard cream-on-cream print
- 1/4 yard green print
- 3/4 yard lining fabric
- 1 yard red print
- Batting 36" x 26"
- 2 strips batting 1" x 22"
- All-purpose thread to match fabrics
- Clear nylon monofilament
- Basic sewing tools and supplies, rotary cutter, mat and ruler

MAKING BAG TOP UNIT

Step 1. Cut one 4 1/2" x 4 1/2" square red print for A.

Step 2. Cut three 2 1/2" by fabric width strips red print; subcut into 2 1/2" square segments for B. You will need 40 red print B squares. Draw a diagonal line from corner to corner on the wrong side of each B square.

Step 3. Cut two 4 1/2" by fabric width strips cream-on-cream print; subcut into 2 1/2" segments for C. You will need 20 C rectangles.

Step 4. Cut one 2 1/2" by fabric width strip cream-on-

Evening Star
8" x 8" Block

cream print; subcut strip into 2 1/2" square segments for D. You will need 12 D squares.

Step 5. Cut four 2 1/2" x 8 1/2" strips for E and two 2 1/2" x 16 1/2" strips for F from green print.

Step 6. Place a B square right sides together with C as shown in Figure 1; stitch on the marked line. Trim away excess to make a 1/4" seam allowance as shown in Figure 2; press B to the right side.

Figure 1
Place a B square right
sides together with C.

Figure 2
Trim away excess to make
a 1/4" seam allowance.

Step 7. Place a second B square on the remaining end of C and stitch as in Step 6. Press and trim off triangle points

to complete one B-C unit as shown in Figure 3. Repeat for 20 B-C units.

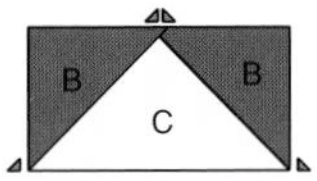

Figure 3
Trim off triangle points to complete 1 B-C unit.

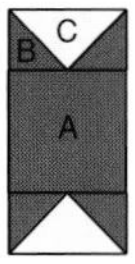

Figure 4
Sew a B-C unit to opposite sides of A.

Step 8. To piece the block, sew a B-C unit to opposite sides of A as shown in Figure 4; press seams toward A.

Step 9. Sew a D square to the ends of two B-C units as shown in Figure 5; repeat. Sew a B-C-D unit to the sides of the A-B-C unit to complete the block as shown in Figure 6; press seams toward A.

Figure 5
Sew a D square to the ends of 2 B-C units.

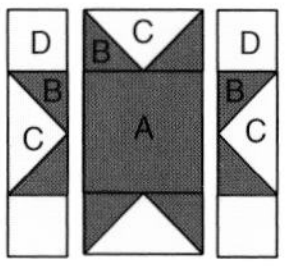

Figure 6
Sew a B-C-D unit to the sides of the A-B-C unit to complete 1 block.

Step 10. Sew E to two opposites sides of the pieced block; press seams toward E. Sew a D square to each end of the remaining E pieces; sew to the remaining sides of the pieced block. Press seams toward D-E.

Step 11. Join three B-C units as shown in Figure 7; repeat for four B-C strips.

Figure 7
Join 3 B-C units.

Step 12. Sew a B-C strip to opposite sides of the pieced center referring to Figure 8; press seams toward E strips.

Figure 8
Sew a B-C strip to opposite sides of the pieced center.

Figure 9
Sew D to each end of the remaining B-C strips and sew to the remaining sides of the pieced center.

Step 13. Sew D to the each end of the remaining B-C strips and sew to the remaining sides of the pieced center as shown in Figure 9; press seams toward E strips.

Step 14. Sew an F strip to one edge of the pieced unit; press seam toward F.

Step 15. Join four B-C units as shown in Figure 10 to make a B-C strip. Sew the strip to the F side of the pieced unit as shown in Figure 11; press seams toward F. Sew the remaining F strip to the remaining long side of the B-C strip to complete the bag front as shown in Figure 12.

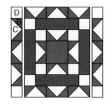

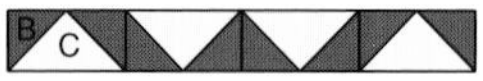

Figure 10
Join 4 B-C units.

Step 16. Cut a 16 1/2" x 22 1/2" rectangle red print for bag back; sew one 22 1/2" side of the bag front to the bag

Figure 11
Sew the B-C strip to the F side of the pieced unit.

Figure 12
Sew the remaining F strip to the remaining long side of the B-C strip to complete the bag front.

back with right sides together and raw edges even to complete the bag unit as shown in Figure 13.

Step 17. Open bag unit and place right side up on the batting piece; pin or baste to hold.

Step 18. Machine-quilt in the ditch of seams using clear nylon monofilament in the top of the machine and all-purpose thread in the bobbin. Bag back is stitched in lines between diagonal corners making a large X to hold batting in place.

16 1/2"

22 1/2"

Figure 13
Sew one 22 1/2" side of the bag front with right sides together and raw edges even to complete the bag unit.

Step 19. When quilting is complete, trim edges even to complete the bag top.

MAKING HANDLES
Step 1. Cut one 3" by fabric width strip red print; remove the selvage edge from each end of the strip. Cut into two equal-size strips.

Step 2. Fold one long edge of each strip 1/4" to the wrong side and press.

Step 3. Fold over opposite long edge of each strip 1" as shown in Figure 14 and press; fold the pressed 1/4" edge over 3/4" on top of the raw edge of the pressed 1" edge and press.

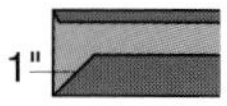

Step 4. Open the pressed edges of each strip and insert a 1"-wide batting strip, aligning batting strip with pressing lines as shown in Figure 15.

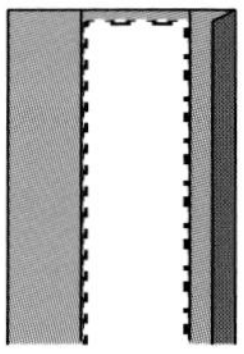

1"

Figure 14
Fold over opposite long edge of each strip 1".

Figure 15
Insert batting strip as shown.

Step 5. Refold pressed edges over the batting, first folding over the 1" edges and overlapping with the 3/4" finished edge; press to make 1"-wide strips.

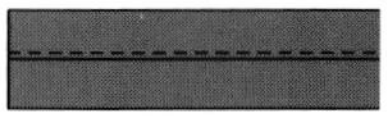

Step 6. Stitch along folded-over edge along center of strips as shown in Figure 16.

Figure 16
Stitch along folded-over edge.

Stitch 1/4" from each outside edge as shown in Figure 17.

Step 7. Square-up ends of each strip to complete handles.

Figure 17
Stitch 1/4" from outside edge.

ATTACHING HANDLES

Step 1. Fold the quilted bag top in half along the width and lay on a flat surface.

Step 2. Measure in 3 3/4" from the raw edge and pin the right side of one end of one handle to the top right side edge of the bag as shown in Figure 18. Measure in 3 1/2" from the side seam and pin the opposite end of the same handle right sides together with bag top edge, again referring to Figure 18. *Note: The right side of the handle strip is the side without the overlapped edge.*

Figure 18
Pin handle ends right sides together with bag top edge as shown.

Step 3. Turn folded bag top over, pin the second handle on bag back as in Step 2 and as shown in Figure 19.

Figure 19
Pin second handle ends on bag back.

Figure 20
Machine-stitch over ends of handles several times to secure in place.

Step 4. Machine-stitch over ends of handles several times to secure in place as shown in Figure 20.

LINING THE BAG

Step 1. Using the quilted bag top as a pattern, cut a lining piece from the lining fabric. *Note: The bag size should be 32 1/2" x 22 1/2" at this time.*

Step 2. Place lining piece right sides together with quilted top. Stitch across top edge of bag, stitching over handle ends.

Step 3. Press seam toward lining and top-stitch close to seam on lining side as shown in Figure 21.

Step 4. Fold bag top and lining sections with right sides together as shown in Figure 22.

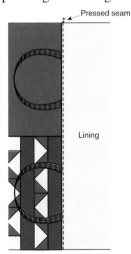

Figure 21
Press seam toward lining and topstitch close to seam on lining side.

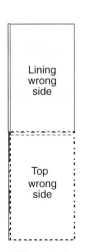

Figure 22
Fold bag top and lining sections with right sides together.

Starting at the bag bottom corner, stitch all around bag top and lining, leaving a 6" opening in the bottom edge of the lining as shown in Figure 23.

Step 5. Trim corners of bag top and lining and trim batting close to seam at top side edge and along bottom corners to reduce bulk.

Step 6. Turn right side out through opening in lining, making sure corners are completely turned.

Step 7. Press seam inside at lining opening edges and machine-stitch opening closed close to edges as shown in Figure 24.

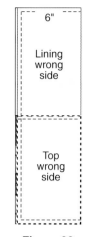

Figure 24
Press seam inside at opening edges and machine-stitch opening closed close to edges.

Figure 23
Stitch all around bag top and lining, leaving a 6" opening in the bottom edge of the lining.

Step 8. Before inserting lining inside bag, press side seam of bag to help make bag lie flat at sides when complete.

Step 9. Insert lining inside bag. Press lining to the inside at the top edge of the bag. Insert iron inside bag and press lining flat as far inside as the iron will slide. Hold the top side of the bag and insert your hand inside the bag to the corners to be sure lining is completely inside and aligned at corners.

Step 10. Topstitch along top edge of bag 1/4"–3/8" from edge using thread to match fabrics or clear nylon monofilament in the top of the machine and all-purpose thread in the bobbin.

Step 11. Choose another area on the bag band and machine-quilt with thread to match fabric or clear nylon monofilament to hold lining layer and bag top together. *Note: This may be in the seam of a strip or 1/4" from a seam or in the center of a strip.* ❖

Evening Star Gift Bag
Placement Diagram
16" x 22"

Colonial Basket Antique Quilt

Green-with-yellow prints were a common combination in fabrics of the later part of the 19th century. This basket quilt uses those colors combined with white set in an unusual layout.

PROJECT NOTES

The basket blocks in the quilt were made in the late 1800s, but were not put together into the quilt top and quilted until much more recently. It appears that the finished quilt was hand-quilted using a polyester batting, dating it to the late 20th century.

The quilt is set in an unusual arrangement with two rows of blocks centered in an upright position. If the quilt is used on a small bed, the side baskets will hang down on the sides in an upright position. It is a nice change from the usual setting.

The green-with-yellow print used in the basket blocks is very faded, but still has plenty of contrast with the white solid background. If you like basket designs, this is a great one.

PROJECT SPECIFICATIONS

Quilt Size: 84 3/4" x 84 3/4"
Block Size: 10" x 10"
Number of Blocks: 36

MATERIALS

- 2 1/4 yards green-with-yellow print
- 7 yards white solid (includes binding)
- Backing 89" x 89"
- Batting 89" x 89"
- White all-purpose thread
- White quilting thread
- 10 yards 1/4"-wide fusible tape
- 1/4" bias bar
- Basic sewing supplies and tools, rotary cutter, mat and ruler, and water-erasable marker or pencil

Colonial Basket
10" x 10" Block

INSTRUCTIONS

Cutting

Step 1. Cut five 8 7/8" by fabric width strips white solid; subcut into eighteen 8 7/8" squares. Cut each square in half on one diagonal to make A triangles; you will need 36 A triangles.

Step 2. Cut 15 strips green-with-yellow print and seven strips white solid 2 7/8" by fabric width; cut strips into 2 7/8" square segments. Cut each square in half on one diagonal to make B triangles; you will need 396 green-with-yellow print and 180 white solid B triangles.

Step 3. Cut three 2 1/2" by fabric width strips white solid; subcut each strip into 2 1/2" square segments for C. You will need 36 C squares.

Step 4. Cut five 6 1/2" by fabric width strips white solid; subcut each strip into 2 1/2" segments for D. You will need 72 D rectangles.

Step 5. Cut three 4 7/8" by fabric width strips white solid; subcut each strip into 4 7/8" square segments. Cut each square in half on one diagonal to make E triangles; you will need 36 E triangles.

Step 6. Cut seven 10 1/2" by fabric width strips white solid; cut strips into 10 1/2" squares for F. You will need 25 F squares.

Step 7. Cut five 15 3/8" x 15 3/8" squares white solid; cut each square on both diagonals to make G triangles as shown in Figure 1. You will need 20 G triangles.

Figure 1
Cut each square on both diagonals to make G triangles.

Step 8. Cut two 8" x 8" squares white solid; cut each square on one diagonal to make H triangles. You will need four H triangles.

Step 9. Cut a 12" by fabric width strip green-with-yellow print; cut into 7/8"-wide bias strips as shown in Figure 2. Join strips on short ends referring to Figure 3 to make 10 1/2 yards 7/8"-wide bias.

Figure 2
Cut the 12" by fabric width strip into 7/8"-wide bias strips as shown.

Figure 3
Join strips on short ends.

Step 10. Cut bias yardage into 9 1/2" lengths for basket handles; you will need 36 handle strips.

Step 11. Cut nine 2 1/4" by fabric width strips white solid for binding.

Piecing Blocks

Step 1. To piece one block, sew a white solid B to a green-with-yellow print B to make a B unit as shown in Figure 4; repeat for five units.

Figure 4
Sew a white solid B to a green-with-yellow print B to make a B unit.

Figure 5
Arrange the B units in rows with 4 B pieces.

Step 2. Arrange the B units in rows with four green-with-yellow print B pieces as shown in Figure 5; join units in rows.

Step 3. Sew C to the dark end of one row referring to Figure 6; join rows to complete the B-C basket section as shown in Figure 7.

Figure 6
Sew C to the dark end of 1 row.

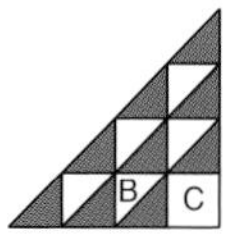

Figure 7
Join rows to complete the B-C basket section.

Step 4. Sew a green-with-yellow print B to the end of each D piece referring to Figure 8; sew to the B-C basket section referring to Figure 9. Press seams toward the D unit.

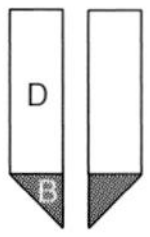

Figure 8
Sew a green-with-yellow print B to the end of each D piece.

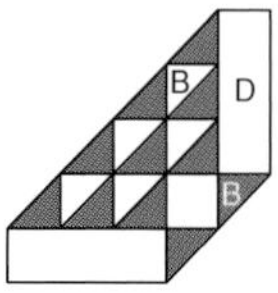

Figure 9
Sew the B-D units to the B-C basket section.

Step 5. Sew E to the pieced section to complete piecing of the bottom section of the block; set aside.

Step 6. Fold one 9 1/2" bias strip in half along length with wrong sides together; stitch along raw edges using a 1/8" seam allowance.

Step 7. Insert the 1/4" bias bar inside strip and press with seam centered and open as shown in Figure 10.

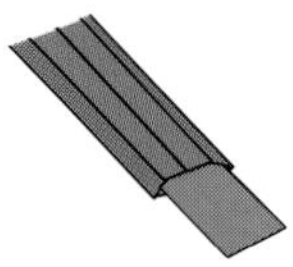

Figure 10
Insert the 1/4" bias bar inside strip and press with seam centered and open.

Step 8. Cut a 9 1/2" length 1/4"-wide fusible tape; fuse to the wrong side of the pressed bias strip.

Step 9. Measure in 3 3/8" from each corner of A and mark using a water-erasable marker or pencil as shown in Figure 11 for handle placement.

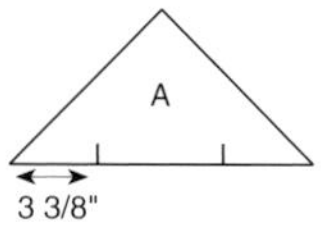

Figure 11
Measure in 3 3/8" from each corner of A and mark.

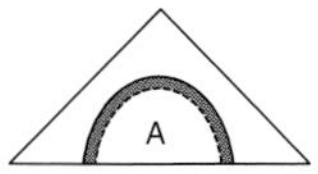

Figure 12
Align the pressed strip with inside edge aligned to placement line on the A triangle.

Step 10. Align the pressed strip with inside edge aligned to placement line on the A triangle as shown in Figure 12; fuse in place to hold. Hand- or machine-appliqué in place.

Step 11. Sew the appliquéd A triangle to the B side of the pieced section to complete one block; press seam toward A. Repeat for 36 blocks.

Step 12. Arrange blocks in diagonal rows with F squares and G and H triangles as shown in Figure 13. ***Note:*** *The quilt shown has an unusual arrangement of the blocks. All blocks may be turned in an upright position if that is your preference.*

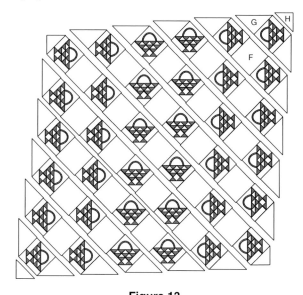

Figure 13
Arrange blocks in diagonal rows with F squares and G and H triangles.

Step 13. Using the water-erasable marker or pencil, mark the quilting design given using the whole design in the F squares, half of the design in the G triangles and one-quarter of the design in the H corner triangles.

Step 14. Sandwich batting between completed top and prepared backing piece; pin or baste layers together to hold flat.

Step 15. Quilt on marked lines and as desired using white hand-quilting thread. *Note: The quilt shown was hand-quilted as marked in Step 13 and in the ditch of all seams using white hand-quilting thread.*

Step 16. When quilting is complete, trim edges even; remove pins or basting.

Step 17. Join the 2 1/4" by fabric width strips white solid on short ends to make one long strip for binding.

Step 18. Fold binding strip with wrong sides together along length and press. Pin to the quilt top edges with raw edges even. Stitch all around, mitering corners and overlapping ends. Turn binding to the backside; hand-stitch in place to finish. ❖

Colonial Basket Antique Quilt
Placement Diagram
84 3/4" x 84 3/4"

Quilting Design

Colonial Basket Pillow Shams

Matching pillow shams add the perfect finish to a bed made with an antique quilt.

PROJECT NOTES

The green-with-yellow print used to make these pillow shams would have matched the colors in the *Colonial Basket* antique quilt perfectly in the late 1800s. Today the quilt is faded and the reproduction prints are bright. Even so, these shams add a perfect accent to the quilt. Any 10" x 10" finished block may be substituted with other fabrics to make shams to match many other quilts.

These shams are very large and can accommodate several pillow sizes. Stitching in the ditch between inside border seams creates a smaller pillow space and larger flange, while stitching in the ditch between outside border seams creates a larger pillow space and a smaller flange.

Purchased pillow shams to match quilts at retail stores are sometimes almost as expensive as the quilt. You can make your own with a little time and less expense.

PROJECT SPECIFICATIONS

Sham Size: 40" x 25 7/8"

Block Size: 10" x 10"

Number of Blocks: 4 (2 for each sham)

MATERIALS

- 1 yard green-with-yellow print
- 2 1/4 yards yard white-on-white print
- 1 3/4 yards white solid for backing
- 1 3/4 yards bleached muslin for lining
- 2 pieces batting 42" x 28"
- White all-purpose thread
- Clear nylon monofilament
- 1 1/4 yards 1/4"-wide fusible tape
- 1/4" bias bar
- Basic sewing supplies and tools, rotary cutter, mat and ruler and water-erasable marker or pencil

INSTRUCTIONS
Cutting

Step 1. Cut two 8 7/8" x 8 7/8" squares white-on-white

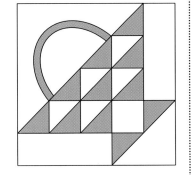

Colonial Basket
10" x 10" Block

print. Cut each square in half on one diagonal to make A triangles; you will need four A triangles.

Step 2. Cut five strips green-with-yellow print and four strips white-on-white print 2 7/8" by fabric width; cut strips into 2 7/8" square segments. Cut each square in half on one diagonal to make B triangles; you will need 136 green-with-yellow print and 112 white-on-white print B triangles.

Step 3. Cut eight 2 1/2" x 2 1/2" squares white solid for C. Cut four 2 1/2" x 2 1/2" squares green-with-yellow print for C.

Step 4. Cut one 6 1/2" x 22" strip white-on-white print; subcut strip into 2 1/2" segments for D. You will need eight D rectangles.

Step 5. Cut two 4 7/8" x 4 7/8" squares white-on-white print. Cut each square in half on one diagonal to make E triangles; you will need four E triangles.

Step 6. Cut four 8" x 8" squares white-on-white print; cut each square on one diagonal to make F triangles. You will need eight F triangles.

Step 7. Cut one 15 3/8" x 15 3/8" square white-on-white print; cut the square in half on both diagonals as shown in Figure 1 to make four G triangles.

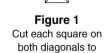

Figure 1
Cut each square on both diagonals to make G triangles.

Step 8. Cut four strips each 1 3/8" x 14 5/8" (H) and 1 3/8" x 30 1/2" (J) green-with-yellow print.

Step 9. Cut four 7/8" x 9 1/2" bias strips green-with-yellow print for basket handles.

Step 10. Cut four strips each 3 1/2" x 20 1/2" (K) and 3 1/2" x 40 1/2" (L) white-on-white print.

Step 11. Cut four 23 1/2" x 26 3/8" rectangles white solid for sham backs.

Step 12. Cut two 42" x 28" rectangles bleached muslin for lining.

Piecing Blocks

Step 1. To piece one block, sew a white-on-white print B

to a green-with-yellow print B to make a B unit as shown in Figure 2; repeat for five units.

Figure 2
Sew a white-on-white print solid B to a green-with-yellow print B to make a B unit.

Figure 3
Arrange the B units in rows with 4 B pieces.

Figure 4
Sew C to the dark end of 1 row.

Step 2. Arrange the B units in rows with four green-with-yellow print B pieces as shown in Figure 3; join units in rows.

Step 3. Sew C to the dark end of one row referring to Figure 4; join rows to complete the B-C basket section as shown in Figure 5.

Figure 5
Join rows to complete the B-C basket section.

Figure 6
Sew a green-with-yellow print B to the end of each D piece.

Figure 7
Sew the B-D units to the B-C basket section.

Step 4. Sew a green-with-yellow print B to the end of each D piece referring to Figure 6; sew to the B-C basket section referring to Figure 7. Press seams toward the D unit.

Step 5. Sew E to the pieced section to complete piecing of the bottom section of the block; set aside.

Step 6. Fold one 9 1/2" bias strip in half along length with wrong sides together; stitch along raw edges using a 1/8" seam allowance.

Step 7. Insert the 1/4" bias bar inside strip and press with seam centered and open as shown in Figure 8.

Step 8. Cut a 9 1/2" length 1/4"-wide fusible tape; fuse to the wrong side of the pressed bias strip.

Figure 8
Insert the 1/4" bias bar inside strip and press with seam centered and open.

Step 9. Measure in 3 3/8" from each corner of A and mark using a water-erasable marker or pencil as shown in Figure 9 for handle placement.

Figure 9
Measure in 3 3/8" from each corner of A and mark.

Figure 10
Align the pressed strip with inside edge aligned to placement line on the A triangle.

Step 10. Align the pressed strip with inside edge aligned to placement line on the A triangle as shown in Figure 10; fuse in place to hold. Hand- or machine-appliqué in place.

Step 11. Sew the appliquéd A triangle to the B side of the pieced section to complete one block; press seam toward A. Repeat for four blocks.

Step 12. Arrange two blocks in diagonal rows with four F and two G triangles as shown in Figure 11. Join the rows to complete the pieced center; repeat for two pieced centers. Press seams away from pieced blocks.

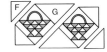

Figure 11
Arrange 2 blocks in diagonal rows with F and G triangles.

Step 13. Sew an H strip to opposite short sides of each pieced center; press seams toward strips. Sew J to opposite long sides of each pieced center; press seams toward strips.

Step 14. Sew a white-on-white print B to a green-with-yellow print B along the diagonal to make a B unit as shown in Figure 2; repeat for 92 B units.

Step 15. Join eight B units to make a pieced strip as shown in Figure 12; press seams in one direction. Repeat for four strips.

Figure 12
Join 8 B units to make a pieced strip.

Step 16. Sew a pieced B strip to opposite short ends of each pieced center; press seams toward the H strips.

Step 17. Join 15 B units to make a pieced strip as shown in Figure 13; press seams in one direction. Sew a green-with-yellow print C to one end and a white-on-white print C to the opposite end, again referring to Figure 13. Repeat for four strips. Sew a strip to opposite long sides of each pieced center; press seams toward J.

Figure 13
Join 15 B units to make a pieced strip. Sew a green-with-yellow print C to 1 end and a white-on-white print C to the opposite end.

Step 18. Sew a K strip to opposite short ends and an L strip to opposite long sides of each pieced center to complete the pieced sham tops; press seams toward K and L.

Finishing Shams

Step 1. Sandwich one batting piece between one pieced sham top and one prepared lining piece; pin or baste layers together to hold flat.

Step 2. Quilt in the ditch of all seams, 3/8" from seams on K and L border strips and double line 3/8" from seams on F and G triangles using clear nylon monofilament in the top of the machine and all-purpose thread in the bobbin.

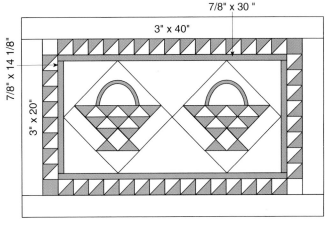

Colonial Basket Pillow Sham
Placement Diagram
40" x 25 7/8"

Step 3. When quilting is complete, trim edges even with pieced tops.

Step 4. Press under 1/4" on one 26 3/8" edge of each sham back piece; press under again 1/2" as shown in Figure 14. Stitch to hem edges.

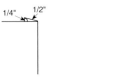
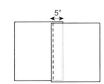

Figure 14
Press under 1/4" on one 26 3/8"-wide end of a sham back piece; press under again 1/2".

Figure 15
Overlap hemmed edges 5".

Step 5. Place two backing pieces right sides together with one quilted pillow sham top, overlapping hemmed edges 5" as shown in Figure 15; pin in place. Sew around the outside edges using a 1/4" seam allowance.

Step 6. Turn to the right side through the back opening; press pillow top.

Step 7. Using clear nylon monofilament in the top of the machine and all-purpose thread in the bobbin, topstitch through all layers between pieced borders and K and L border strips to make a flange. ***Note:** If you would like to use these shams on smaller pillows, you may stitch in the seams between the H and J strips and the pieced B border strips.*

Step 8. Insert the pillow through back opening to use. ❖

Star Flower Antique Quilt

Lemon yellow and white solids create a quilt that is still vibrant after 70 years of use.

PROJECT NOTES

Yellow is not a favorite color of fabric for contemporary designers and manufacturers. It is hard to find nice yellow solids or prints. The yellow used in the *Star Flower* quilt is a lovely lemon shade, and even though the quilt has been in use for many years, it looks almost as good as new. It was hand-pieced and hand-quilted.

The quilt tells me that its maker was a precise stitcher. The points of each star are perfect and the center circle is perfectly round. When hung with light behind it, I could see that a few seams were pressed in different directions along the borders and that there was one dark piece of thread quilted between the top and batting layers. These little things can't be detected when the quilt is on a bed.

I discovered the pattern in *Bold and Beautiful Quilts* from Aunt Martha's Studio. There is no copyright date on the booklet, but the price of $1.25 is written in pencil on the top corner. I would guess it is a reprint of earlier patterns from the 1930s.

The copy with the pattern states: "Star Flower, a unique utilization of an age-old favorite needlecraft—puffing portions of a quilt. Raised and puffed petals of a flower against a star make this quilt worthy of note."

The C template given with that Star Flower pattern is a bit different in shape from the one we used, but works the same way. This pattern is much easier than a typical star design because you don't have to worry about points meeting in the center. Simply piece the design and gather the C pieces until it lies flat before appliquéing the A circle on top.

PROJECT SPECIFICATIONS

Quilt Size: 79 1/2" x 95"

Size of Block: 12" x 12"

Number of Blocks: 20

MATERIALS

- 5 yards yellow solid (includes binding)
- 5 yards white solid
- Backing 84" x 99"
- Batting 84" x 99"
- White all-purpose thread
- White hand-quilting thread
- Heat-resistant template material
- Spray starch
- Basic sewing supplies and tools, water-erasable marker or pencil and hole punch or awl

Star Flower
12" x 12" Block

CUTTING INSTRUCTIONS

Step 1. Cut two strips each 4" x 82" and 4" x 98" white solid along length of fabric; set aside for borders.

Step 2. Cut four strips each 4" x 82" and 4" x 98" yellow solid along length of fabric; set aside for borders.

Step 3. Cut fourteen 4" by fabric width strips from remaining width white solid; subcut into 4" square segments for D. You will need 80 D squares.

Step 4. Prepare templates using pattern pieces given; make a hole in templates at dots on pieces B and C using a hole punch or awl. Cut fabric patches as directed on each piece, transferring dots to patches using a water-erasable marker or pencil. *Note: Use fabric width left after cutting border strips and D squares before cutting into remaining full fabric width.*

Step 5. Cut five 6 1/4" by fabric width strips white solid; subcut strips into 6 1/4" square segments. Cut each square on both diagonals to make E triangles; you will need 80 E triangles.

Step 6. To piece one block, join two B pieces with C, stopping stitching at the marked dots as shown in Figure 1 to make a B-C unit. *Note: Stitching may be done by hand or machine.* Repeat for four B-C units.

Figure 1
Join 2 B pieces with C, stopping stitching at the marked dots as shown to make a B-C unit.

Figure 2
Set an E piece between the points of B, stopping stitching at the marked dots on B to make a B-C-E unit.

Step 7. Set an E piece between the points of B, stopping stitching at the marked dots on B to make a B-C-E unit as shown in Figure 2; repeat for four B-C-E units.

Step 8. Join the B-C-E units to complete the star shape as shown in Figure 3, stopping stitching at marked dots. *Note: The C pieces will not lie flat yet.*

Step 9. Set a D square into each corner as shown in Figure 4, stopping stitching at marked dots.

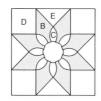

Figure 3
Join the B-C-E units to complete the star shape.

Figure 4
Set a D square into each corner.

Step 10. Thread a needle and knot one end of the thread. Hand-stitch 1/8" from raw edges of C; pull thread to gather piece and secure as shown in Figure 5. Cut thread leaving a 2" tail. Repeat on all C pieces. Adjust gathers, if necessary, to make the pieced section lie flat.

Step 11. Remove the seam allowance from the A template; cut a heat-resistant template this size.

Step 12. Center the new A template on the wrong side of each fabric A piece; trace to mark seam allowance using the water-erasable marker or pencil.

Step 13. Spray a little spray starch on a piece of waste paper. Using your finger, spread a little starch on the seam allowance area of one marked A piece as shown in Figure 6.

Figure 5
Hand-stitch 1/8" from raw edges of C; pull thread to gather piece and secure.

Figure 6
Using your finger, spread a little starch on the seam allowance area of 1 marked A piece.

Star Flower Antique Quilt
Placement Diagram
79 1/2" x 95"

Step 14. Place the heat-resistant A template on the wrong side of a fabric A piece; using an iron, press starched seam over template to make a perfect circle. Remove the template; repeat on all A pieces.

Step 15. Center and hand-appliqué the A piece over the ends of B and gathered C pieces to complete one block; repeat for 20 blocks.

Step 16. Cut three 12 1/2" by fabric width strips white solid; subcut into 4" segments for sashing strips. Cut one more sashing strip from remaining white solid; you will need 31 sashing strips.

Step 17. Cut two 4" by fabric width strips yellow solid; subcut strips into 4" square segments for sashing squares. You will need 12 sashing squares.

Step 18. Join four blocks with three sashing strips to make a block row as shown in Figure 7; press seams toward sashing strips. Repeat for five block rows.

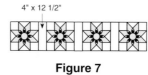

Figure 7
Join 4 blocks with 3 sashing strips to make a block row.

Figure 8
Join 4 sashing strips with 3 sashing squares to make a sashing row.

Step 19. Join four sashing strips with three sashing squares to make a sashing row as shown in Figure 8; press seams toward sashing squares. Repeat for four sashing rows.

Step 20. Join the block rows with the sashing rows, beginning and ending with a block row; press seams toward sashing rows.

Step 21. Sew a shorter white solid strip with right sides together along length between two same-length yellow solid strips; repeat to make top and bottom border strips. Press seams toward yellow solid strips. Repeat with longer white and yellow solid strips to make two side border strips.

Step 22. Center and sew the shorter border strips to the top and bottom and longer border strips to opposite long sides, mitering corners; trim excess fabric at corners to 1/4" as shown in Figure 9.

Figure 9
Trim excess fabric on wrong side of mitered corners.

Step 23. Mark the sashing strips and borders with the quilting design given using a water-erasable marker or pencil. Mark the block corners and sashing squares with the quilting design given.

Step 24. Sandwich batting between the completed top and prepared backing piece; pin or baste layers together to hold.

Step 25. Quilt on marked lines by hand or machine. *Note: The quilt shown was hand-quilted using designs given and 1/4" from seams in the B and E pieces and in concentric circles in A using white hand-quilting thread.*

Step 26. When quilting is complete, trim excess batting and backing edges even with quilted top. Place a plate on each corner and trim to make rounded corners.

Step 27. Cut nine strips yellow solid 2 1/4" by fabric width. Join strips on short ends to make one long strip for binding.

Step 28. Fold binding strip with wrong sides together along length and press. Pin to the quilt top edges with raw edges even. Stitch all around, overlapping ends. Turn binding to the backside; hand-stitch in place to finish. ❖

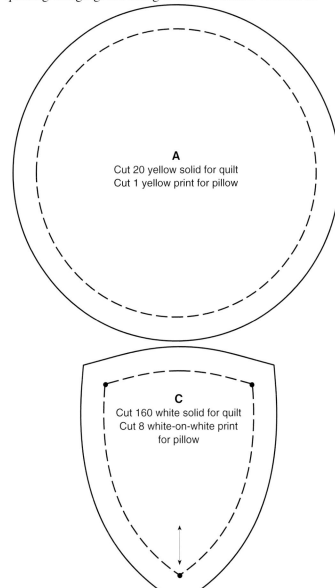

A
Cut 20 yellow solid for quilt
Cut 1 yellow print for pillow

C
Cut 160 white solid for quilt
Cut 8 white-on-white print
for pillow

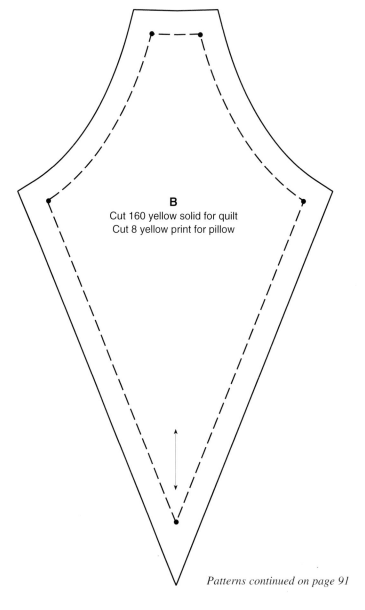

B
Cut 160 yellow solid for quilt
Cut 8 yellow print for pillow

Patterns continued on page 91

Star Flower Pillow

Make one or more pillows to coordinate with your antique quilt.

PROJECT NOTES

Ruffled pillows dress up a bed, couch or chair. This one-block pillow matches the *Star Flower* antique quilt. Although not made with the same fabric, the pale yellows blend well with the original quilt. Borders could be added to the block to create another larger pillow to add even more color accents and comfort to the ensemble.

PROJECT SPECIFICATIONS

Pillow Size: 12" x 12" without ruffle

Size of Block: 12" x 12"

Number of Blocks: 1

Star Flower
12" x 12" Block

MATERIALS

- 1/4 yard yellow print
- 1/2 yard white-on-white print
- 5/8 yard yellow-and-white stripe
- 14" x 14" square muslin for lining
- 2 rectangles backing 9 1/2" x 12 1/2"
- Batting 14" x 14"
- White all-purpose thread
- Yellow hand-quilting thread
- Clear nylon monofilament
- Heat-resistant template material
- Spray starch
- 12" x 12" pillow form
- Basic sewing supplies and tools, water-erasable marker or pencil and hole punch or awl

CUTTING INSTRUCTIONS

Step 1. Prepare templates for pieces A, B and C using patterns given for *Star Flower* antique quilt on page 83.

Step 2. Make a hole in templates at dots on pieces B and C, using a hole punch or awl. Cut fabric patches as directed on each piece for pillow, transferring dots to patches using a water-erasable marker or pencil.

Step 3. Cut four 4" x 4" squares white-on-white print for D.

Step 4. Cut one 6 1/4" x 6 1/4" square white-on-white print. Cut the square on both diagonals to make E triangles; you will need 4 E triangles.

Step 5. To piece one block, join two B pieces with C,

stopping stitching at the marked dots as shown in Figure 1 to make a B-C unit. *Note: Stitching may be done by hand or machine.* Repeat for four B-C units.

Figure 1	**Figure 2**
Join 2 B pieces with C, stopping stitching at the marked dots as shown to make a B-C unit.	Set an E piece between the points of B, stopping stitching at the marked dots on B to make a B-C-E unit.

Step 6. Set an E piece between the points of B, stopping stitching at the marked dots on B to make a B-C-E unit as shown in Figure 2; repeat for four B-C-E units.

Step 7. Join the B-C-E units to complete the star shape as shown in Figure 3, stopping stitching at marked dots. *Note: The C pieces will not lie flat yet.*

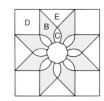

Figure 3	**Figure 4**
Join the B-C-E units to complete the star shape.	Set a D square into each corner.

Step 8. Set a D square into each corner as shown in Figure 4, stopping stitching at marked dots.

Step 9. Thread a needle and knot one end of the thread. Hand-stitch 1/8" from raw edges of C; pull thread to gather piece and secure as shown in Figure 5. Cut thread leaving a 2" tail. Repeat on all C pieces. Adjust gathers, if necessary, to make the pieced section lie flat.

Figure 5
Hand-stitch 1/8" from raw edges of C; pull thread to gather piece and secure.

Step 10. Remove the seam allowance from the A template; cut a heat-resistant template this size.

Step 11. Center the new A template on the wrong side of fabric A piece; trace to mark seam allowance using the water-erasable marker or pencil.

Step 12. Spray a little spray starch on a piece of waste paper. Using your finger, spread a little starch on the seam allowance area of marked A piece as shown in Figure 6.

Step 13. Place the heat-resistant A template on the wrong side of the fabric A piece; using an iron, press starched seam over template to make a perfect circle. Remove the template.

Figure 6
Using your finger, spread a little starch on the seam allowance area of the marked A piece.

Step 14 Center and hand-appliqué the A piece over the ends of B and gathered C pieces to complete the block.

Step 15. Sandwich batting between the completed block and prepared lining piece; pin or baste layers together to hold.

Step 16. Quilt in the ditch of seams and 3/8" from seams in the B, D and E pieces using clear nylon monofilament in the top of the machine and all-purpose thread in the bobbin. Hand-quilt 1/4" from edge of A using yellow hand-quilting thread.

Step 17. When quilting is complete, trim excess batting and backing edges even with quilted block.

Step 18. Cut three strips each 1 1/2" and 5 1/2" by fabric width yellow-and-white stripe and three strips 2 1/2" by fabric width white-on-white print.

Step 19. Sew a white-on-white print strip between a 1 1/2"-wide and a 5 1/2"-wide yellow-and-white stripe strip with right sides together along length; press seams away from center strip. Repeat for three strip sets. Join the strip sets on the short ends to make a tube; press seams open.

Step 20. Fold the tube with wrong sides together and matching raw edges as shown in Figure 7; press. Divide the tube into four equal parts and mark with a pin or water-erasable marker or pencil.

Figure 7
Fold the tube with wrong sides together and matching raw edges.

Step 21. Stitch two parallel lines of gathering stitches (large machine stitches) close to raw edge of folded tube; pull stitches to gather evenly.

Step 22. Pin the gathered ruffle to quilted pillow top block, matching marked line or pins to corners; evenly distribute gathering on each side between corners; machine-baste to hold in place.

Step 23. Press under 1/4" on one 12 1/2" edge of each backing piece; press under again 1/2" as shown in Figure 8. Stitch to hem edges.

Step 24. Place two backing pieces right sides together with the quilted pillow top block, tucking ruffle between

Figure 8
Press under 1/4" on one 12 1/2" edge of each backing piece; press under again 1/2".

Figure 9
Overlap backing pieces as shown.

layers and overlapping hemmed edges 5" as shown in Figure 9; pin in place. Sew around the outside edges using a 1/4" seam allowance.

Step 25. Turn to the right side through the back opening; press pillow top and insert pillow form to finish. ❖

Star Flower Pillow
Placement Diagram
12" x 12"
(without ruffle)

Job's Troubles Antique Quilt

The antique quilt, Job's Troubles, *requires set-in seams and precise piecing of points. Although hand piecing is recommended for novice stitchers, more experienced stitchers may successfully use machine-piecing methods.*

PROJECT NOTES

As with most antique quilts, when examined, it seems accuracy in piecing is inconsistent. The quilt shown is no exception. The pink rectangle pieces B on the inside blocks are all the same size, but those used on the outside blocks are almost 3/4" narrower. Of course, this means that the C pieces joining these areas are not equilateral triangles as in the blocks. This really doesn't matter because these pieces do not get stitched together with other blocks. Our instructions use the same-size B and C pieces throughout.

The quilt uses a very thick batting, but is still heavily quilted. I wonder how the quilter did it. The batting has migrated in lumps in areas where the quilting is less than 1/2" apart. This gives the quilt lots of texture.

This quilt design was shown in Barbara Brackman's *Encyclopedia of Pieced Quilt Patterns* with several variations and different names—Brunswick Star, Rolling Stone and Chained Star are a few examples. Job's Troubles seems like the most appropriate name. It was published in the magazine, *Modern Priscilla,* begun in 1897. This magazine was a mail-order source for patterns during the early 1900s until it was bought by *Needlecraft—The Home Arts Magazine* in 1930. The shirting prints along with the navy print clearly date the quilt at the turn of the century.

PROJECT SPECIFICATIONS

Quilt Size: 77" x 79 1/2"

Block Size: 15 7/8" x 15"

MATERIALS

- Scraps navy, burgundy, black, gray and brown prints and plaids for dark A pieces
- Scraps pink and white prints and plaids for light A pieces

- 1/2 yard each 3 different white shirting prints for borders and C pieces
- 2/3 yard tan stripe for borders and side triangles
- 2 yards dark pink print
- 4 yards muslin (includes binding)
- Backing 81" x 84"
- Batting 81" x 84"
- All-purpose thread to match fabrics
- White hand-quilting thread
- Basic sewing tools and supplies, rotary cutter, mat and ruler, water-erasable marker or pencil and hole punch or awl

Job's Troubles
15 7/8" x 15" Block

INSTRUCTIONS

Step 1. Prepare templates for A–E using pattern pieces given; cut as directed on each piece.

Step 2. Using a hole punch or awl, make a hole in the points of the A, C and D templates as shown in Figure 1. Place the templates on the wrong side of the corresponding fabric patches. Using a sharp lead pencil, make a mark through the holes to mark seam joints as shown in Figure 2.

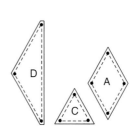

Figure 1
Using a hole punch, cut a hole in the points of the A, C and D templates.

Figure 2
Make a mark through the holes to mark seam joints.

Step 3. Sew a dark print A to a light print A, starting and

ending seams at the marked dots as shown in Figure 3, securing seams at the beginning and end; set in a muslin A as shown in Figure 4. Repeat for three units. Join the pieced units to create a star unit as shown in Figure 5, again starting and ending seams at the marked dots; press seams in one direction. Set in a muslin A between dark and light print A pieces, again referring to Figure 5. Press center seam in a swirling pattern as shown in Figure 6. Repeat for 36 star units.

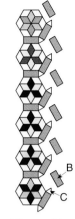

Figure 3
Sew a dark print A to a light print A, starting and ending seams at the marked dots.

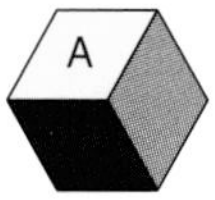

Figure 4
Set in a muslin A.

Figure 5
Join the pieced units to create a star unit.

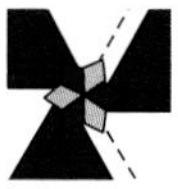

Figure 6
Press center seam in a swirling pattern.

Step 4. Sew C to each end of 33 B pieces to make a B-C unit as shown in Figure 7; press seams toward B. Set aside six units.

Figure 7
Make a B-C unit.

Step 5. Sew a B-C unit to three straight sides of a star unit as shown in Figure 8; set in B between the B-C units, again referring to Figure 8 and starting and stopping at marked dots to complete a Job's Troubles block. Press seams toward B. Repeat for nine blocks.

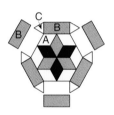

Figure 8
Sew B-C to 3 straight sides of a star unit; set in B pieces.

Step 6. Add B and C pieces to nine star units as shown in Figure 9 to create partial blocks. Cut three partial blocks in half as shown in Figure 10.

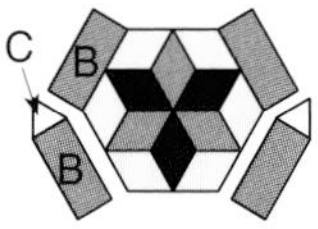

Figure 9
Add B and C pieces to a star unit to create a partial block.

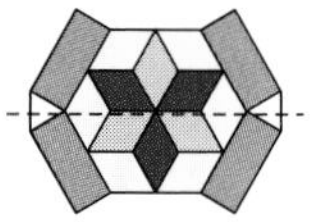

Figure 10
Cut 3 partial blocks in half.

Step 7. Join three blocks, two partial blocks and two half-partial blocks to make an A row as shown in Figure 11; repeat for three A rows. Press seams toward blocks.

Step 8. Join six star units with five B pieces to make a B row as shown in Figure 12; repeat for three B rows. Press seams toward B pieces.

Step 9. Sew a B-C unit to one edge of each star unit in

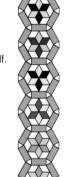

Figure 11
Make an A row as shown.

Figure 12
Make a B row as shown.

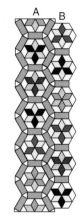

Figure 13
Sew B-C unit to 1 edge of each star unit in 1 B row; set in B pieces.

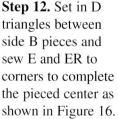

Figure 14
Join the A and B rows.

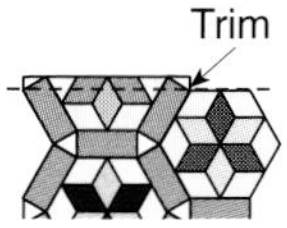

Figure 15
Trim the A rows even with the B rows.

one B row as shown in Figure 13; set in B pieces on the adjacent edges, again referring to Figure 13. Trim ends even with star units.

Step 10. Join the A and B rows referring to Figure 14 for positioning of rows; press seams toward the A rows.

Step 11. Trim the A rows even with the B rows as shown in Figure 15 to complete the top and bottom of the pieced center.

Step 12. Set in D triangles between side B pieces and sew E and ER to corners to complete the pieced center as shown in Figure 16.

Step 13. Cut and piece two strips tan stripe 2" x 70 1/2"

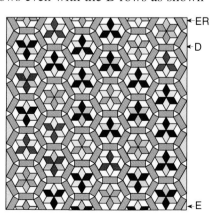

Figure 16
Set in D triangles; add E and ER triangles to corners.

and two strips white shirting print 2 1/2" x 70 1/2"; sew the tan strips and then the white strips to the top and bottom of the pieced center. Press seams toward strips.

Step 14. Cut and piece two strips one white shirting print 2" x 80" and two strips another white shirting print 2 1/2" x 80". Sew the narrower strips and then the wider strips to opposite long sides to complete the pieced top.

Step 15. Sandwich batting between the completed top and prepared backing piece; pin or baste layers together to hold.

Step 16. Quilt as desired by hand or machine. ***Note:*** *The quilt shown was heavily hand-quilted using white quilting thread in a continuous swirling pattern with lines about 1/2" apart over the entire quilt.*

Step 17. When quilting is complete, trim excess batting and backing edges even with quilted top.

Step 18. Cut eight strips muslin 2 1/4" by fabric width. Join strips on short ends to make one long strip for binding.

Step 19. Fold binding strip with wrong sides together along length and press. Pin to the quilt top edges with raw edges even. Stitch all around, mitering corners and overlapping ends. Turn binding to the backside; hand-stitch in place to finish. ❖

Job's Troubles Antique Quilt
Placement Diagram
77" x 79 1/2"

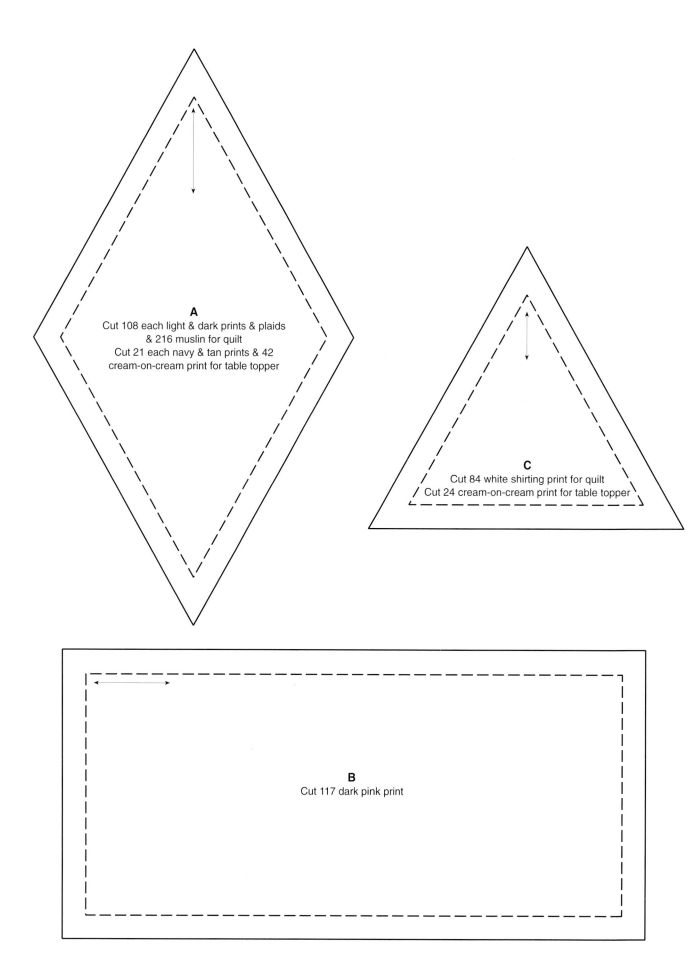

A
Cut 108 each light & dark prints & plaids
& 216 muslin for quilt
Cut 21 each navy & tan prints & 42
cream-on-cream print for table topper

C
Cut 84 white shirting print for quilt
Cut 24 cream-on-cream print for table topper

B
Cut 117 dark pink print

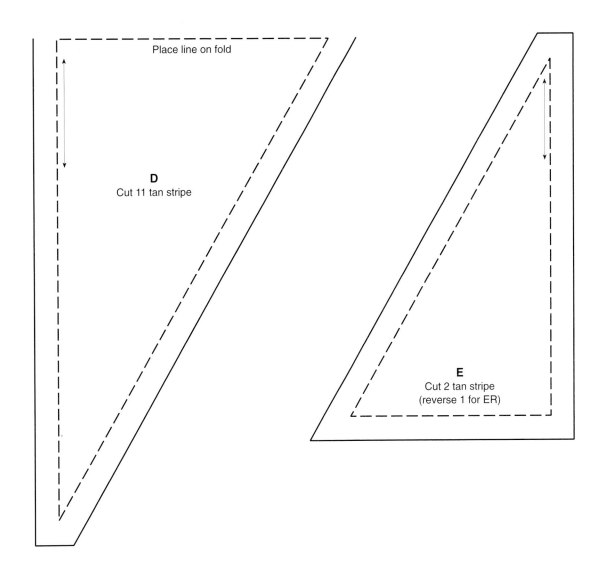

Place line on fold

D
Cut 11 tan stripe

E
Cut 2 tan stripe
(reverse 1 for ER)

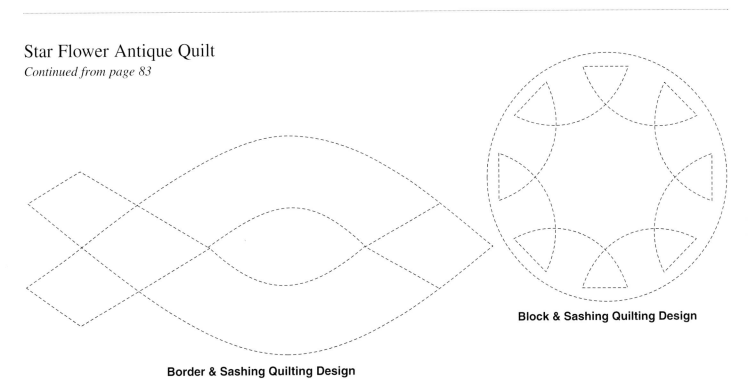

Star Flower Antique Quilt
Continued from page 83

Border & Sashing Quilting Design

Block & Sashing Quilting Design

Job's Troubles Table Topper

Set-in seams can be machine-stitched successfully with careful stitching and by starting and ending seams at the marked seam allowance.

PROJECT NOTES

You may choose to use the templates given, or use a special angled ruler designed for cutting 60-degree angle diamond shapes. There are several rulers on the market that may be used to create diamond shapes and eliminate the need for templates. Each ruler comes packaged with its own special instructions that can be applied to the template shapes given.

The table topper shown was created to coordinate with the *Job's Troubles Antique Quilt* on page 86. When the quilt is placed on a bed with the topper on a round cardboard-base decorator table, it is hard to tell that the fabrics used in the topper were not the same fabrics used in the antique quilt.

PROJECT SPECIFICATIONS

Quilt Size: 37 1/2" x 40"

Block Size: 15 7/8" x 15"

MATERIALS

- 1/2 yard tan print
- 1/2 yard cream-on-cream print
- 5/8 yard dark pink print
- 3/4 yard navy print (includes binding)
- Backing 42" x 44"
- Batting 42" x 44"
- All-purpose thread to match fabrics
- Clear nylon monofilament
- Basic sewing tools and supplies, rotary cutter, mat and ruler, water-erasable marker or pencil and hole punch or awl

Job's Troubles
15 7/8" x 15" Block

INSTRUCTIONS

Step 1. Prepare templates using pattern pieces given on page 90 for A and C.

Step 2. Fold the cream-on-cream print with right sides together and selvage edges even. Place the A template on the fabric as shown in Figure 1. Place a ruler on top of the template, aligning edge. Using a rotary cutter, cut through both layers as shown in Figure 2.

Figure 1
Place the A template on
the fabric as shown.

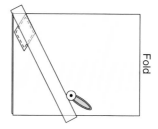

Figure 2
Place a straightedge ruler on top of the
template, aligning edge. Using a rotary
cutter, cut through both layers.

Step 3. Place the ruler on the opposite side of the template and cut as in Step 2 to make a strip. Lay the A template on the strip and cut as shown in Figure 3. Repeat to cut 42 A pieces.

Figure 3
Lay the A template on
the strips and cut.

Figure 4
Cut C pieces from
leftover ends.

Step 4. Cut C pieces from leftover ends as shown in Figure 4.

Step 5. Cut remaining navy and tan print A pieces using the template given or referring to Steps 2 and 3.

Step 6. Cut three strips pink print 6 1/4" by fabric width; subcut into 3" segments for B; you will need 30 B pieces.

Step 7. Using a hole punch or awl, make a hole in the points of the A and C templates as shown in Figure 5. Place the templates on the wrong side of the corresponding fabric patches. Using a sharp lead pencil, make a mark through the holes to mark seam joints as shown in Figure 6.

Step 8. Sew a navy print A to a tan print A, starting and ending seams at the marked dots as shown in Figure 7, securing seams at the beginning and end; set in a cream-on-cream print A as shown in Figure 8. Repeat for three units. Join the pieced units to create a star unit as shown in Figure 9, again starting and ending seams at the marked

Figure 5
Cut a hole in the points of the A and C templates.

Figure 6
Make a mark through the holes to mark seam joints.

Figure 7
Sew a navy print A to a tan print A, starting and ending seams at the marked dots.

Figure 8
Set in a cream-on-cream print A.

Figure 9
Join the pieced units to create a star unit.

dots; press seams in one direction. Set in a cream-on-cream print A between navy and tan print A pieces, again referring to Figure 9. Press center seam in a swirling pattern as shown in Figure 10. Repeat for seven star units.

Figure 10
Press center seam in a swirling pattern.

Step 9. Sew C to each end of 12 B pieces as shown in Figure 11. Sew a B-C unit to three straight sides of a star unit as shown in Figure 12; set in B pieces between the B-C units, starting and stopping at marked dots to complete a Job's Troubles block. Repeat for three blocks.

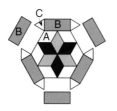

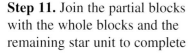

Figure 11
Sew C to each end of B.

Figure 12
Sew B-C to 3 straight sides of a star unit; set in B pieces.

Step 10. Add B pieces and a B-C unit to three star units as shown in Figure 13 to create partial blocks.

Step 11. Join the partial blocks with the whole blocks and the remaining star unit to complete

Figure 13
Add B pieces and a B-C unit to 3 star units.

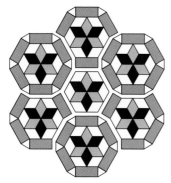

Figure 14
Join the partial blocks with the whole blocks and the remaining star unit to complete the pieced top.

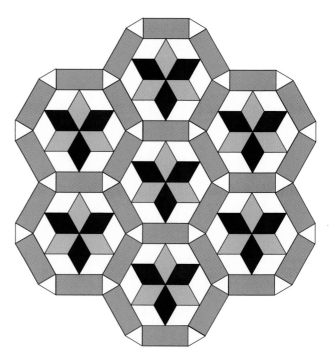

Job's Troubles Table Topper
Placement Diagram
37 1/2" x 40"

the pieced top as shown in Figure 14. Press seams toward B pieces.

Step 12. Sandwich batting between the completed top and prepared backing piece; pin or baste layers together to hold.

Step 13. Quilt in the ditch of seams and 1/4"–3/8" from seams inside all B and the navy print A pieces using clear nylon monofilament in the top of the machine and all-purpose thread in the bobbin.

Step 14. When quilting is complete, trim excess batting and backing edges even with quilted top.

Step 15. Cut four strips navy print 2 1/4" by fabric width. Join strips on short ends to make one long strip for binding.

Step 16. Fold binding strip with wrong sides together along length and press. Pin to the quilt top edges with raw edges even. Stitch all around, mitering corners and overlapping ends. Turn binding to the backside; hand-stitch in place to finish. ❖

Mrs. Brown's Choice Antique Quilt

Indigo-dyed fabrics were popular in the late 1800s and were quite durable when compared to other fabric dyes which caused fabric deterioration. The indigo on this quilt has not faded, and, except for the wear on the border strips, the quilt looks fresh and new.

PROJECT NOTES

Navy and white or indigo and white is my favorite color combination. I have several antique quilts using this combination. Navy-with-white dots was a popular fabric choice of quilters in the mid-1800s. The graphic designs used to create the quilts are clearly visible when only two colors are used.

This pattern can be found using several other names, Sawtooth Patchwork (Ladies Art Co., No. 271), Another Sawtooth (*The Perfect Patchwork Primer,* 1973) and Mrs. Brown's Choice (Needlecraft Supply, 1938), but this quilt was made earlier than any of these sources.

The quilt is hand-pieced and heavily hand-quilted. Its maker was not trying to make a quick quilt and probably cut each individual piece using templates. Today the pieces for this quilt can easily be rotary-cut and stitched together by machine.

PROJECT SPECIFICATIONS

Quilt Size: 81" x 91 1/2"

Block Size: 10 1/2" x 10 1/2"

Number of Blocks: 28

MATERIALS

- 3 3/4 yards navy-with-white print
- 6 1/2 yards muslin
- Backing 85" x 96"
- Batting 85" x 96"
- All-purpose thread to match fabrics
- Cream hand-quilting thread
- Basic sewing tools and supplies, rotary cutter, mat and ruler and water-erasable marker or pencil

Mrs. Brown's Choice
10 1/2" x 10 1/2" Block

INSTRUCTIONS

Step 1. Cut 28 squares muslin 11" x 11" for fill-in blocks.

Step 2. Cut 14 strips 4" by fabric width navy-with-white print; subcut strips into 4" square segments for A. You will need 140 A squares.

Step 3. Cut seven 4 3/8" by fabric width strips each navy-with-white print and muslin; subcut strips into 4 3/8" square segments. Cut each square on one diagonal to make B triangles; you will need 112 B triangles of each fabric.

Step 4. Cut 25 strips 2 1/4" by fabric width muslin; subcut strips into 2 1/4" square segments for C. You will need 448 C squares. Draw a diagonal line from corner to corner on the wrong side of each C square.

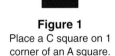

Figure 1
Place a C square on 1
corner of an A square.

Step 5. Place a C square on one corner of an A square as shown in Figure 1; stitch on the drawn line.

Step 6. Trim seam to 1/4" beyond stitched line; press C to the right side with seam toward C as shown in Figure 2. Repeat on the remaining corners of A, placing C as shown in Figure 3 to complete an A-C unit as shown in Figure 4. Repeat for 112 A-C units.

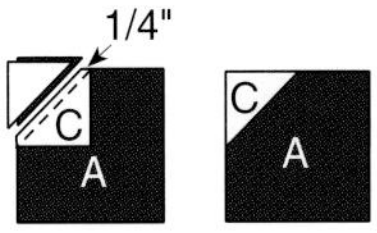

Figure 2
Trim seam to 1/4" beyond
stitched line; press C to the
right side with seam toward C.

Figure 3
Place C on remaining
corners of A.

Figure 4
Complete an A-C
unit as shown.

Figure 5
Sew a muslin B to a
navy-with-white print B
along the diagonal to
complete a B unit.

Step 7. Sew a muslin B to a navy-with-white print B along the diagonal to complete a B unit as shown in Figure 5; repeat for 112 B units. Press seams toward darker fabric.

Step 8. Arrange the A-C units with the B units and A in rows as shown in Figure 6. Join units in rows; join rows to complete one block. Repeat for 28 blocks.

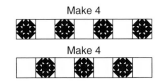

Figure 6
Arrange the A-C units with
the B units and A in rows.

Figure 7
Join pieced blocks with muslin
fill-in blocks to make a row.

Step 9. Join four pieced blocks with three muslin fill-in blocks to make a row as shown in Figure 7; press seams away from pieced blocks. Repeat for four rows.

Step 10. Join three pieced blocks with four muslin fill-in blocks to make a row, again referring to Figure 7; press seams away from pieced blocks. Repeat for four rows.

Step 11. Join the block rows referring to the Placement Diagram for positioning; press seams in one direction.

Step 12. Cut and piece four strips each muslin and two strips each navy-with-white print 1 3/4" x 84" and 1 3/4" x 95". Sew a same-size navy-with-white print strip between two muslin strips with right sides together along length; repeat to make two combined strips in each size. Press seams toward darker fabric.

Step 13. Center and sew the shorter strips to the top and bottom of the pieced center, and longer strips to opposite sides, mitering corners as shown in Figure 8; trim excess seam at miter to 1/4" and press to one side.

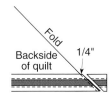

Figure 8
Miter corners.

Step 14. Mark the fill-in blocks with the quilting pattern given or as desired using a water-erasable marker or pencil.

Step 15. Sandwich batting between the completed top and prepared backing piece; pin or baste layers together to hold.

Step 16. Using cream hand-quilting thread, quilt on

Mrs. Brown's Choice Antique Quilt
Placement Diagram
81" x 91 1/2"

marked lines and with four diagonal lines 3/8" apart and then 3/4" apart on pieced blocks and into borders as shown in Figure 9.

Step 17. When quilting is complete, trim excess batting and backing edges even with quilted top.

Figure 9
Quilt as shown.

Step 18. Cut nine strips navy-with-white print 2 1/4" by fabric width. Join strips on short ends to make one long strip for binding.

Step 19. Fold binding strip with wrong sides together along length and press. Pin to the quilt top edges with raw edges even. Stitch all around, mitering corners and overlapping ends. Turn binding to the backside; hand-stitch in place to finish. ❖

Quilting Design

Mrs. Brown's Choice
Table Runner

Reversing the placement of the darks and lights changes the appearance of a design.

PROJECT NOTES

It is easy to find reproduction prints in the navy-with-white color combination. The fabric used to make this runner to accompany the *Mrs. Brown's Choice* antique quilt matches the shade of blue in the quilt perfectly. Two of the blocks in the runner are pieced in reverse color order from the quilt. This emphasizes a different part of the block design.

PROJECT SPECIFICATIONS

Runner Size: 42 1/2" x 18" (includes binding)

Block Size: 10 1/2" x 10 1/2"

Number of Blocks: 3

MATERIALS

- 1/2 yard muslin
- 1 1/4 yards navy-with-white print (includes binding)
- Backing 47" x 22"
- Batting 47" x 22"
- All-purpose thread to match fabrics
- Clear nylon monofilament
- Basic sewing tools and supplies, rotary cutter, mat and ruler

Mrs. Brown's Choice
10 1/2" x 10 1/2" Block

Mrs. Brown's Choice
10 1/2" x 10 1/2" Block

INSTRUCTIONS

Step 1. Cut nine 4" x 4" squares navy-with-white print and ten 4" x 4" squares muslin for A.

Step 2. Cut six 4 3/8" x 4 3/8" squares each navy-with-white print and muslin. Cut each square on one diagonal to make B triangles; you will need 12 B triangles of each fabric.

Step 3. Cut two 2 1/4" by fabric width strips each muslin and navy-with-white print; subcut strips into 2 1/4" square segments for C. You will need 32 each muslin and navy-with-white print C squares. Draw a diagonal line from corner to corner on the wrong side of each C square.

Step 4. Place a muslin C square on one corner of a navy-with-white print A square as shown in Figure 1; stitch on the drawn line.

Figure 1
Place a C square on 1 corner of an A square.

Step 5. Trim seam to 1/4" beyond stitched line; press C to the right side with seam away from A as shown in Figure 2. Repeat on the remaining corners of A, placing C as shown in Figure 3 to complete an A-C unit as shown in Figure 4. Repeat for eight A-C units with navy-with-white print A squares and eight with muslin A squares. Set aside four navy-with-white print A-C units for border corners.

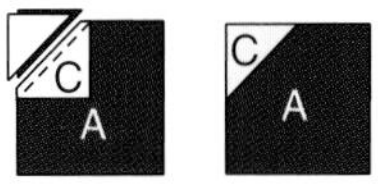

Figure 2
Trim seam to 1/4" beyond stitched line; press C to the right side with seam toward C.

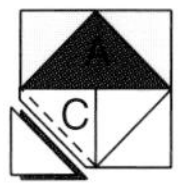

Figure 3
Place C on remaining corners of A.

Figure 4
Complete an A-C unit as shown.

Step 6. Sew a muslin B to a navy-with-white print B along the diagonal to complete a B unit as shown in Figure 5; repeat for 12 B units. Press seams toward darker fabric.

Figure 5
Sew a muslin B to a navy-with-white print B along the diagonal to complete a B unit.

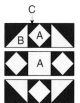

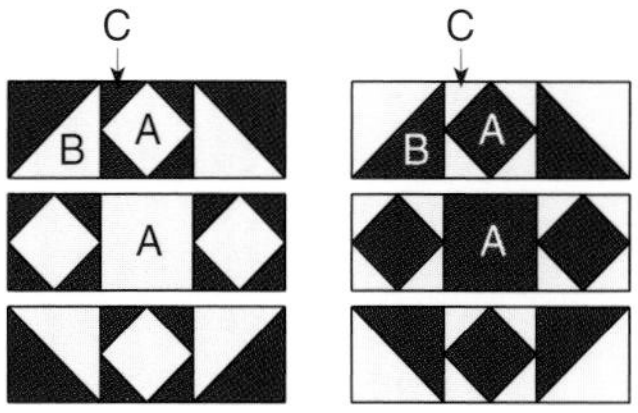

Make 2   Make 1

Figure 6
Arrange the A-C units with the B units and A in rows.

Step 7. Arrange the A-C units with the B units and A in rows as shown in Figure 6. Join units in rows; join rows

to complete one muslin block and two navy-with-white print blocks.

Step 8. Cut two 2 1/4" x 11" strips navy-with-white print strips for sashing. Join the blocks with the sashing strips with the muslin block in the center; press seams toward sashing strips.

Step 9. Cut two strips each 4" x 11" and 4" x 35 1/2" navy-with-white print for borders. Sew the longer strips to opposite long sides; press seams toward strips.

Step 10. Sew the A-C units set aside in Step 5 to each end of the 4" x 11" border strips as shown in Figure 7. Sew these strips to opposite short ends of the pieced center to complete the runner top.

Figure 7
Sew an A-C unit to each
end of a 4" x 11" strip.

Step 11. Sandwich batting between the completed top and prepared backing piece; pin or baste layers together to hold.

Step 12. Quilt in the ditch of seams, with lines 3/8" apart on the edges of the border strips or as desired using clear nylon monofilament in the top of the machine and all-purpose thread in the bobbin.

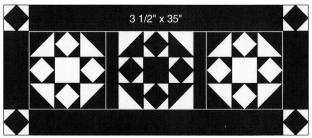

Mrs. Brown's Choice Runner
Placement Diagram
42 1/2" x 18" (includes binding)

Step 13. When quilting is complete, trim excess batting and backing edges even with quilted top.

Step 14. Cut four strips navy-with-white print 2 1/4" by fabric width. Join strips on short ends to make one long strip for binding.

Step 15. Fold binding strip with wrong sides together along length and press. Pin to the runner top edges with raw edges even. Stitch all around, mitering corners and overlapping ends. Turn binding to the backside; hand-stitch in place to finish. ❖

Shadow Star Antique Quilt

Some of the blocks in this old quilt may be faded, but the design is still fresh and makes a wonderful bed quilt.

PROJECT NOTES

I don't know any of this quilt's history. I would guess that it was made in the late 1800s from looking at the fabrics. The fabrics in some of the blocks are quite faded, while a few blocks appear to be close to their original color. The batting is very thin, and the backing and binding fabric very loosely woven. The quilting stitches are uneven, and the knots show on the top. In spite of its faults, I really like the design and the color combination.

This pattern would work with almost any fabric combination whether you choose two, three or more fabrics. The quilt shown uses all solids. If I were choosing fabric, I would never choose all solids nor these colors, but they work in this quilt in a rather striking manner.

PROJECT SPECIFICATIONS

Quilt Size: 68 1/2" x 92"

Block Size: 21 1/2" x 21 1/2"

Number of Blocks: 12

MATERIALS

* 1 3/8 yards green solid
* 2 1/2 yards brick solid
* 3 1/4 yards muslin
* Backing 73" x 96"
* Batting 73" x 96"
* Neutral color all-purpose thread
* Cream hand-quilting thread
* Basic sewing supplies and tools, rotary cutter, mat and ruler

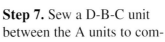

Shadow Star
21 1/2" x 21 1/2" Block

INSTRUCTIONS

Step 1. Prepare templates using pattern pieces given on pages 106–108; cut as directed on each piece for quilt for one block; repeat for 12 blocks.

Step 2. To piece the block, join one muslin and two dark green solid A pieces as shown in Figure 1; repeat with two muslin and three dark green solid A pieces referring to Figure 2.

Figure 1
Join 1 muslin and 2 dark green solid A pieces.

Figure 2
Join 2 muslin and 3 dark green solid A pieces.

Figure 3
Join the pieced A units with a dark green solid A to complete 1 A unit.

Step 3. Join the pieced A units with a dark green solid A to complete one A unit as shown in Figure 3; repeat for eight A units. Press seams away from dark green solid A pieces.

Step 4. Join four A units with four B triangles to make the block center as shown in Figure 4; press seams toward B.

Step 5. Sew an A unit to the end of each B triangle in the block center as shown in Figure 5.

Figure 4
Join 4 A units with 4 B triangles to make the block center.

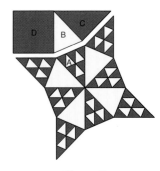

Figure 5
Sew an A unit to the end of each B triangle.

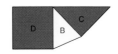

Figure 6
Sew D to B to C as shown.

Step 6. Sew D to B to C as shown in Figure 6; repeat for four units.

Step 7. Sew a D-B-C unit between the A units to complete the block as shown in Figure 7; press seams toward darker fabrics. Repeat for 12 blocks.

Figure 7
Sew a D-B-C unit between the A units.

Step 8. Cut nine strips muslin 2 1/2" x 22" for sashing. Join four blocks with three strips to make a row as shown in Figure 8; press seams toward strips. Repeat for three rows.

Step 9. Cut and piece two strips muslin 2 1/2" x 92 1/2". Join the rows with the strips to complete the pieced top; press seams toward strips.

Step 10. Sandwich batting between the completed top and prepared backing piece; pin or baste layers together to hold flat.

Step 11. Quilt as desired by hand or machine. *Note: The quilt shown was hand-quilted 1/4" from the ditch of seams in the pieced A units and in parallel lines spaced 1/4" apart in 2" intervals in the B, C and D pieces using cream hand-quilting thread.*

Step 12. Cut eight 2 1/4" by fabric width strips muslin. Join the strips on short ends to make one long strip for binding.

Step 13. Fold binding strip with wrong sides together along length and press. Pin to the quilt top edges with raw edges even. Stitch all around, mitering corners and overlapping ends. Turn binding to the backside; hand-stitch in place to finish. ❖

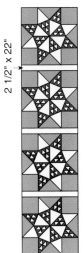

2 1/2" x 22"

Figure 8
Join 4 blocks
with 3 strips to
make a row.

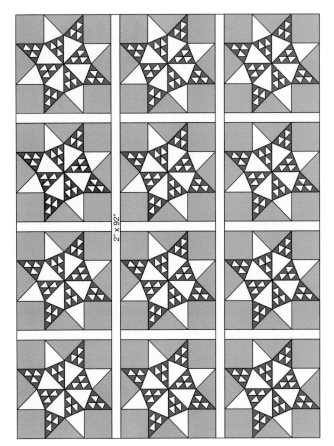

2" x 92"

Shadow Star Antique Quilt
Placement Diagram
68 1/2" x 92"

Shadow Star
Table Topper

Border a large block and add braided cord to make a table topper with style.

PROJECT NOTES

I tried to match the fabrics used in the antique Shadow Star quilt using the fabrics in my collection. My colors are pretty close to the original colors, but I moved the colors to different positions to create a different look.

This table topper could be used on a nightstand next to a bed, or it could be used as a wall quilt to hang on the wall above the bed.

The pattern is not an easy one, but can be machine-pieced because of the straight seams. A bit of skill is needed to make precise set-in seams, but this is not as difficult as it may seem as long as you stop stitching at the end of the seam, not at the end of the piece.

PROJECT SPECIFICATIONS

Quilt Size: 30 1/2" x 30 1/2"

Block Size: 21 1/2" x 21 1/2"

Number of Blocks: 1

MATERIALS

- 1/3 yard brick solid
- 5/8 yard muslin
- 1 1/8 yards dark green solid
- Backing 34" x 34"
- Batting 34" x 34"
- Neutral color all-purpose thread
- Clear nylon monofilament
- Dark green and cream machine-quilting thread
- 3 1/2 yards 1/2"-wide natural cotton braided cord with lip
- Basic sewing supplies and tools, rotary cutter, mat and ruler and zipper foot

Shadow Star
21 1/2" x 21 1/2" Block

INSTRUCTIONS

Step 1. Prepare templates using pattern pieces given; cut as directed on each piece.

Figure 1
Join 1 brick solid
and 2 dark green
solid A pieces.

Step 2. To piece the block, join one brick solid and two dark green solid A pieces as shown in Figure 1; repeat with two brick solid and three dark green solid A pieces referring to Figure 2.

Figure 2
Join 2 brick solid
and 3 dark green
solid A pieces.

Figure 3
Join the pieced A units
with a dark green solid
A to complete 1 A unit.

Step 3. Join the pieced A units with a dark green solid A to complete one A unit as shown in Figure 3; repeat for eight A units. Press seams away from dark green solid A pieces.

Step 4. Join four A units with four B triangles to make the block center as shown in Figure 4; press seams toward B.

Step 5. Sew an A unit to the end of each B triangle in the block center as shown in Figure 5.

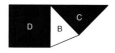

Figure 4
Join 4 A units with 4
B triangles to make
the block center.

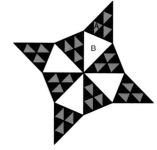

Figure 5
Sew an A unit to the
end of each B triangle.

Step 6. Sew D to B to C as shown in Figure 6; repeat for four units.

Figure 6
Sew D to B to C as shown.

Step 7. Sew a D-B-C unit be-tween the A units to complete the block as shown in Figure 7; press seams toward darker fabrics.

Step 8. Cut two strips each

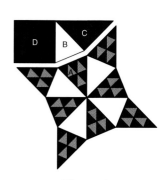

Figure 7
Sew a D-B-C unit
between the A units.

2" x 22" and 2" x 25" muslin. Sew the shorter strips to opposite sides and longer strips to the top and bottom of the pieced center; press seams toward strips.

Step 9. Cut two strips each 1 1/4" x 25" and 1 1/4" x 26 1/2" brick solid. Sew the shorter strips to opposite sides and longer strips to the top and bottom of the pieced center; press seams toward strips.

Step 10. Cut two strips each 2 3/4" x 26 1/2" and 2 3/4" x 31" dark green solid. Sew the shorter strips to opposite sides and longer strips to the top and bottom of the pieced center; press seams toward strips.

Step 11. Sandwich batting between the completed top and prepared backing piece; pin or baste layers together to hold flat.

Step 12. Quilt as desired by hand or machine, stopping quilting before the last border strips. ***Note:*** *The quilt shown was machine-quilted in the ditch of seams using clear nylon monofilament in the top of the machine and all-purpose thread in the bobbin. Dark green machine-quilting thread was used to quilt 3/8" from seams on the C and D pieces and dark green solid border strips, and cream machine-quilting thread was used to quilt 3/8" from the seams on the B pieces and muslin strips.*

Step 13. When quilting is complete, trim batting only even with quilt top; remove pins or basting. Trim backing 1/2" larger than quilt top all around; fold the excess backing back to last quilting lines on the backside and pin to hold out of the way as shown in Figure 8.

Figure 8
Fold the excess backing back to last quilting lines on the backside and pin to hold out of the way.

Step 14. Pin the 1/2"-wide natural cotton braided cord to the edge of the quilted top, matching the lip on the cord to the raw edge of the quilted top. Attach zipper foot and machine-baste in place, clipping the cord lip at corners as shown in Figure 9 and overlapping beginning and end as shown in Figure 10. Turn the cord to the right side to check placement; adjust as necessary. Machine-stitch in place.

Step 15. Unpin backing piece; press under edges 1/2" all around. Pin folded edge of backing to the backside edge,

Figure 9
Clip the cord lip at corners.

Figure 10
Overlap beginning and end of cord.

Shadow Star Table Topper
Placement Diagram
30 1/2" x 30 1/2"

covering the lip of the cord as shown in Figure 11; press and pin to hold. Hand-stitch in place.

Step 16. Finish hand- or machine-quilting in the dark green solid border strips as desired to finish. ❖

Figure 11
Pin folded edge of backing to the backside edge covering the lip of the cord.

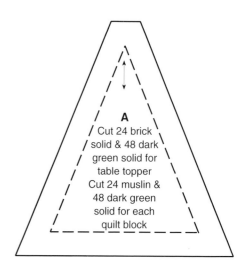

A
Cut 24 brick solid & 48 dark green solid for table topper
Cut 24 muslin & 48 dark green solid for each quilt block

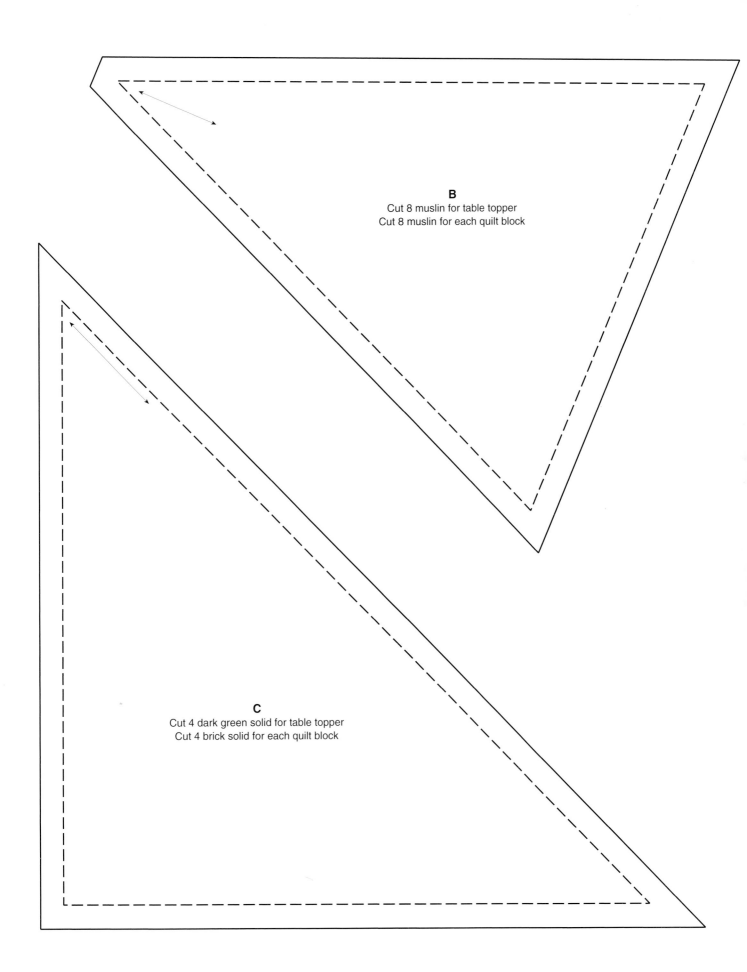

B
Cut 8 muslin for table topper
Cut 8 muslin for each quilt block

C
Cut 4 dark green solid for table topper
Cut 4 brick solid for each quilt block

D
Cut 4 dark green solid for table topper
Cut 4 brick solid for each quilt block

Mrs. Taft's Choice Antique Quilt

One block design can be pieced in so many different ways. This old quilt has a neat pattern which can be made easily by adding seams.

PROJECT NOTES

The antique *Mrs. Taft's Choice* quilt was made using sashing strips, which interrupt the design formed when blocks are joined butted against each other. A very thick batting was used to make a warm quilt. It was hand-quilted with very large stitches, which doesn't seem to diminish the quilt in any way.

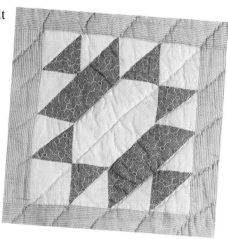

The block in the quilt was made by setting the B squares into the corners of the completed block. Our new version of this pattern, used to make *Sunflower Stars* on page 112, eliminates the set-in seams but adds more seams to match when piecing the block.

The pattern was first printed in *Happy Hours Magazine* at the turn of the century. Most of the blocks in this quilt use fabrics from the late 1800s, but a few of the lighter-colored blocks were made with fabrics from the early 1900s. Whether the quilt was put together by the same person at a later date, we will never know, but it is interesting to see how the fabrics from two very different time periods successfully work together to make a warm and inviting quilt.

PROJECT SPECIFICATIONS

Quilt Size: 75" x 87"

Block Size: 9"x 9"

Number of Blocks: 42

MATERIALS

- One 7" x 18" rectangle 42 different-color fabrics—predominately brown, beige and rust prints, plaids or checks
- 3 yards muslin

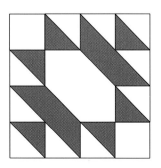

Mrs. Taft's Choice
9" x 9" Block

- 3 5/8 yards pink-and-white stripe
- Backing 79" x 91"
- Batting 79" x 91"
- All-purpose thread to match fabrics
- Cream hand-quilting thread
- Basic sewing tools and supplies, rotary cutter, mat and ruler

INSTRUCTIONS

Step 1. Prepare templates for pieces C and D using patterns given (pages 111 and 115); cut as directed on each piece, using one 7" x 18" colored rectangle for all colored pieces in each block.

Step 2. Cut three 3 1/8" x 3 1/8" squares from each colored rectangle for A; cut each square in half on one diagonal to make six A triangles of each fabric.

Step 3. Cut seventeen 3 1/8" by fabric width strips muslin; subcut strips into 3 1/8" square segments. Cut each square in half on one diagonal to make muslin A triangles. You will need 420 muslin A triangles.

Step 4. Cut six 2 3/4" by fabric width strips muslin; subcut into 2 3/4" square segments for B. You will need 84 muslin B squares.

Step 5. To piece one block, sew a muslin A triangle to the ends of D as shown in Figure 1; repeat.

Step 6. Sew two colored A triangles to each end of C as shown in Figure 2.

Figure 1
Sew a muslin A triangle
to the ends of D.

Figure 2
Sew 2 colored A triangles
to each end of C.

Step 7. Sew a colored A to a muslin A along the diagonal; sew a muslin A to adjacent sides of the colored A to make a corner unit as shown in Figure 3. Repeat for two corner units.

Figure 3
Sew a muslin A to adjacent
sides of the colored A to
make a corner unit.

Step 8. Sew an A-D unit to opposite sides of the A-C unit; add an A corner unit to the D side of the pieced unit as shown in Figure 4.

Step 9. Set a B square into each remaining corner to complete one block. Repeat for 42 blocks; press seams toward darker fabrics.

Step 10. Cut four strips pink-and-white stripe 9 1/2" by fabric width; subcut into 3 1/2" segments for sashing strips. You will need 48 strips.

Step 11. Join seven blocks and eight sashing strips to make a row as shown in Figure 5; press seams toward strips. Repeat for six rows.

Step 12. Cut seven 3 1/2" x 87 1/2" strips pink-and-white stripe along the length of the fabric for long sashing strips.

Step 13. Join the pieced rows with the long sashing strips to complete the pieced top; press seams toward strips.

Figure 4
Add an A corner unit to the D side of the pieced unit.

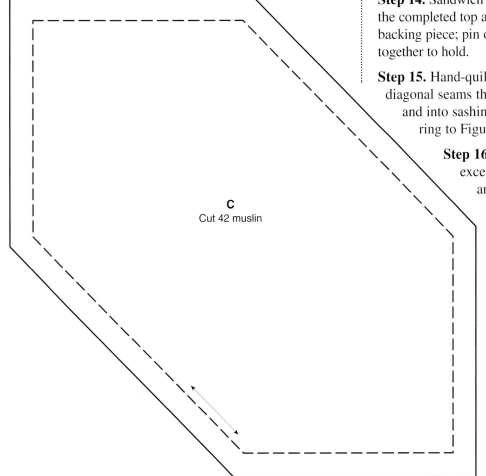

Figure 5
Join 7 blocks and 8 sashing strips to make a row.

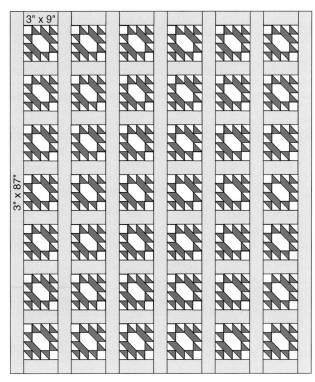

Mrs. Taft's Choice Antique Quilt
Placement Diagram
75" x 87"

Step 14. Sandwich batting between the completed top and prepared backing piece; pin or baste layers together to hold.

Step 15. Hand-quilt in the ditch of diagonal seams through blocks and into sashing strips referring to Figure 6 using cream hand-quilting thread.

Figure 6
Quilt through the blocks and sashing strips following diagonal seams on blocks.

Step 16. When quilting is complete, trim excess batting 1/2" smaller than quilt top all around. Trim backing edges even with quilted top.

Step 17. Turn edges of backing and quilt top under 1/4" and press. Machine-stitch close to edge through all layers to finish. ❖

Pattern continued on page 115

C
Cut 42 muslin

Sunflower Stars

Change the fabrics used and the orientation of a single unit and a whole new design emerges.

PROJECT NOTES

The antique Mrs. Taft's Choice pattern was the design basis for this quilt. The block was divided into 16 equal parts and pieced using triangles and squares. The orientation of the B squares and the A units differs slightly from the original quilt as shown in Figure 1. This change creates the purple points of the star design formed when the blocks are stitched together as shown in Figure 2.

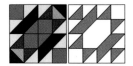

Figure 1
The drawings show the original block design and the varied block design. Notice that the squares and triangle units in the corners are the only difference in placement, but the original block doesn't have as many seams.

Figure 2
The purple star points are formed when 4 blocks are joined as shown.

Figure 3 shows what would happen to this same quilt if the units were placed the same as in the antique *Mrs. Taft's Choice* quilt. Figure 4 shows yet another alternative when the A units are turned with a different color on the corners. There are lots of possible design arrangements.

Figure 3
A different design is formed when 4 blocks arranged like the Mrs. Taft's Choice antique quilt are joined using these fabrics.

Figure 4
When the A units are turned with the alternate color in the corners, yet another design is formed when 4 blocks are joined.

The antique quilt had sashing between the blocks, so no secondary design was formed. Every block used different prints and seemed more of a scrap quilt than a planned one.

When I was working in the design phase of making this quilt, I invited my daughter, Sarah, to help me. I offered to pay her so she would have some money for her Christmas shopping. We made different-color drawings of the blocks and actually stitched them in different colors before we arrived at our final result.

Sarah helped me cut and stitch the quilt, and we enjoyed several days together sewing. Although she is not interested in making quilts, I know that she has learned the skills she needs to cut and stitch accurately. She has also learned about proper pressing and the importance of pressing seams in the right direction. Some day when she does find she really is interested in making quilts, she will be ready to begin on her own. I hope I live to see that day!

PROJECT SPECIFICATIONS

Quilt Size: 80" x 92"

Block Size: 12" x 12"

Number of Blocks: 30

MATERIALS

- 1 1/4 yards purple print
- 1 1/2 yards red print
- 1 3/4 yards yellow mottled
- 2 3/8 yards dark green print (includes binding)
- 2 3/4 yards sunflower print
- Backing 84" x 96"
- Batting 84" x 96"
- All-purpose thread to match fabrics
- Gold machine-quilting thread
- Basic sewing tools and supplies, rotary cutter, mat and ruler

Sunflower Star
12" x 12" Block

INSTRUCTIONS

Step 1. Cut three strips each sunflower and red prints, six strips purple print and 12 strips each dark green print and yellow mottled 3 7/8" by fabric width; subcut each strip into 3 7/8" square segments. Cut each square on one diagonal to make A triangles; you will need 60 each sunflower and red prints, 120 purple print and 240 each dark green print and yellow mottled A triangles.

Step 2. Cut 10 strips sunflower print 3 1/2" by fabric width; subcut strips into 3 1/2" square segments for B. You will need 120 B squares.

Step 3. Sew a dark green print A to a red print A to make a green/red A unit referring to Figure 5; repeat for 60 units.

Make 120   Make 120   Make 60   Make 60

Figure 5
Join A triangles to make A units as shown.

Step 4. Sew a dark green print A to a yellow mottled A to make a green/yellow A unit referring to Figure 5; repeat for 120 A units.

Step 5. Sew a purple print A to a yellow mottled A to make a purple/yellow A unit referring to Figure 5; repeat for 120 A units.

Step 6. Sew a dark green print A to a sunflower print A to make a green/sunflower A unit referring to Figure 5; repeat for 60 A units.

Step 7. To piece one block, arrange the A units with a B square to make an X row as shown in Figure 6. Join to make a row; press seams in one direction. Repeat for 60 X rows.

Figure 6
Arrange the A units with a B square to make an X row.

Figure 7
Arrange the A units with a B square to make a Y row.

Step 8. Arrange the A units with a B square to make a Y row as shown in Figure 7. Join to make a row; press seams in one direction. Repeat for 60 Y rows.

Step 9. Arrange two X rows with two Y rows to make one Sunflower Star block as shown in Figure 8. Join rows to complete the block; press seams in one direction. Repeat for 30 blocks.

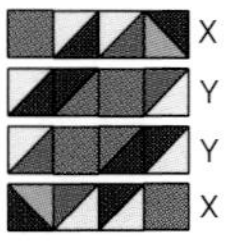

Figure 8
Arrange 2 X rows with 2 Y rows to make 1 Sunflower Star block.

Step 10. Arrange five blocks to make an A row as shown in Figure 9; repeat for three rows. Press seams in one direction.

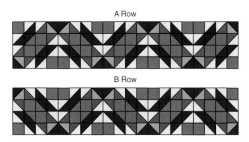

A Row

B Row

Figure 9
Join blocks as shown to make A and B rows.

Step 11. Arrange five blocks to make a B row, again referring to Figure 9; repeat for three rows. Press seams in one direction.

Step 12. Join the rows, alternating A and B rows, referring to the Placement Diagram, to complete the pieced center. Press seams in one direction.

Step 13. Cut and piece two strips each 1 1/2" x 60 1/2" and 1 1/2" x 74 1/2" red print. Sew the shorter strips to the top and bottom and longer strips to opposite long sides; press seams toward strips.

Step 14. Cut four strips each fabric 2 1/2" by fabric

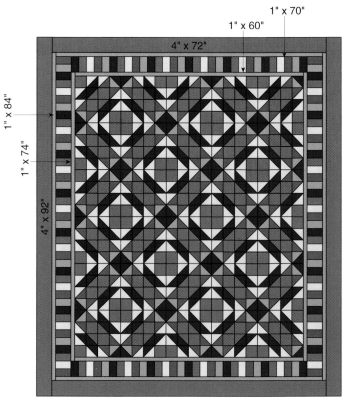

Sunflower Stars
Placement Diagram
80" x 92"

width. Sew one strip of each fabric with right sides together along length to make a strip set as shown in Figure 10; press seams in one direction. Repeat for four strip sets.

Figure 10
Sew 1 strip of each fabric with right sides together along length to make a strip set.

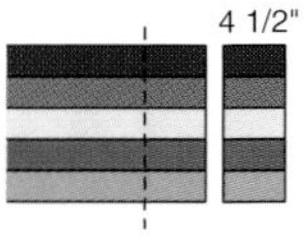

Figure 11
Subcut strip sets into 4 1/2" segments.

Step 15. Subcut strip sets into 4 1/2" segments as shown in Figure 11; you will need 32 segments.

Step 16. Join seven segments on the 4 1/2" edges to make a long strip; remove four strips from one end as shown in Figure 12. Repeat for two strips; sew a strip to the top and bottom of the pieced center referring to the Placement Diagram for positioning. Press seams toward red print strips.

Figure 12
Remove 4 strips from 1 end of the strip unit.

Step 17. Join nine segments as in Step 16, except remove three strips from one end and one strip from the opposite end as shown in Figure 13. Repeat for two strips; sew a

Figure 13
Remove 3 strips from 1 end and 1 strip from the other end of the strip unit.

Mrs. Taft's Choice Antique Quilt

Continued from page 111

strip to opposite long sides of the pieced center, again referring to the Placement Diagram for positioning. Press seams toward red print strips.

Step 18. Cut and piece two strips each 1 1/2" x 70 1/2" and 1 1/2" x 84 1/2" red print. Sew the shorter strips to the top and bottom and longer strips to opposite long sides; press seams toward strips.

Step 19. Cut and piece two strips each 4 1/2" x 72 1/2" and 4 1/2" x 92 1/2" sunflower print; sew the shorter strips to the top and bottom and longer strips to opposite sides of the pieced center. Press seams toward strips.

Step 20. Sandwich batting between the completed top and prepared backing piece; pin or baste layers together to hold.

Step 21. Quilt as desired by hand or machine. *Note: The quilt shown was professionally machine-quilted in an allover floral/leaf design using gold machine-quilting thread.*

Step 22. When quilting is complete, trim excess batting 1/2" smaller than quilt top all around. Trim backing edges even with quilted top.

Step 23. Cut nine strips dark green print 2 1/4" by fabric width. Join strips on short ends to make one long strip for binding.

Step 24. Fold binding strip with wrong sides together along length and press. Pin to the quilt top edges with raw edges even. Stitch all around, mitering corners and overlapping ends. Turn binding to the backside; hand-stitch in place to finish. ❖

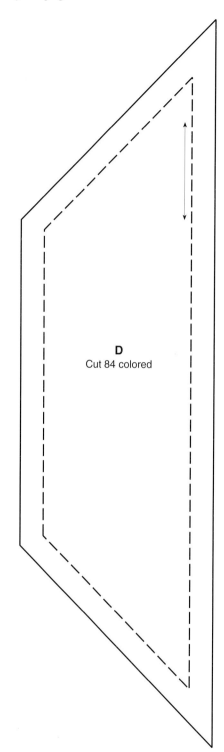

D
Cut 84 colored

Snowball & Nine-Patch Antique Quilt

The Snowball & Nine-Patch design is lost in the sea of white background in this soft, old quilt.

PROJECT NOTES

Orange is not a popular color in quiltmaking; you have only to make a visit to your local fabric store and search for orange to see that. There are Halloween prints in orange, but few others.

Back in the 1930s, orange was a popular color along with a very strange green color and pastel prints. Today there are lots of reproduction prints from that era, but only a few of those are orange.

The Snowball and Nine-Patch design is not as recognizable in this quilt because of the white setting squares. So much white makes it look like the orange squares and triangles are sparsely placed on the quilt in a strange pattern. Upon close inspection, it is easy to find the blocks. Also note that the blocks in the bottom row are in a different position than the remaining rows. Our Placement Diagram and instructions show the quilt with rows arranged in one direction.

This is one of the most simple designs, and alternating setting blocks with pieced blocks cuts down the piecing by half. Use quick-cutting and -piecing methods, and you can whip up this quilt top in a weekend.

PROJECT SPECIFICATIONS

Quilt Size: 63 3/4" x 76 1/2"

Block Size: 9" x 9"

Number of Blocks: 30

MATERIALS

- 1 1/2 yards orange solid
- 5 yards white solid
- Backing 68" x 80"
- Batting 68" x 80"
- Neutral color all-purpose thread
- White hand-quilting thread
- Basic sewing supplies and tools, rotary cutter, mat and ruler

Snowball & Nine-Patch
9" x 9" Block

INSTRUCTIONS

Step 1. Cut eight 5" by fabric width strips white solid; subcut into 5" square segments for A. You will need 60 A squares.

Step 2. Cut twelve 2" by fabric width strips orange solid; subcut strips into 2" square segments for B. You will need 240 B squares. Draw a diagonal line from corner to corner on the wrong side of each B square.

Step 3. Place a B square right sides together on one corner of A as shown in Figure 1; stitch on the marked line.

 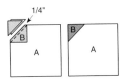

Figure 1
Place a B square right sides together on 1 corner of A.

Figure 2
Trim seam to 1/4"; press B to the right side.

Figure 3
Sew B on each corner of A to complete an A-B Snowball unit.

Step 4. Trim seam to 1/4"; press B to the right side as shown in Figure 2. Repeat on each corner of A to complete an A-B Snowball unit as shown in Figure 3. Repeat to make 60 A-B Snowball units.

Step 5. Cut 15 strips white solid and 12 strips orange solid 2" by fabric width.

Step 6. Sew an orange solid strip between two white solid strips with right sides together along length to make a white/orange/white strip set; press seams toward the orange solid strip. Repeat for six white/orange/white strip sets.

Step 7. Sew a white solid strip between two orange solid strips with right sides together along length to make an orange/white/orange strip set; press seams toward the orange solid strips. Repeat for three strip sets.

Step 8. Subcut strip sets into 2" segments as shown in Figure 4; you will need 120 white/orange/white and 60 orange/white/orange segments.

Figure 4
Subcut strip sets into 2" segments.

Figure 5
Join segments to make a Nine-Patch unit.

Step 9. Sew an orange/white/orange segment between two white/orange/white segments to make a Nine-Patch unit as shown in Figure 5; repeat for 60 Nine-Patch units.

Step 10. Sew a Nine-Patch unit to an A-B Snowball unit as shown in Figure 6; repeat. Join the units to complete one block as shown in Figure 7. Repeat for 30 blocks.

Figure 6
Sew a Nine-Patch unit to an A-B Snowball unit.

Figure 7
Join units to complete 1 block.

Step 11. Cut five 9 1/2" by fabric width strips white solid; subcut strips into 9 1/2" square segments for D. You will need 20 D squares.

Step 12. Cut five 14" x 14" squares white solid; cut each square in half on both diagonals to make E triangles as shown in Figure 8.

Figure 8
Cut the 14" x 14" squares in half on both diagonals to make E triangles.

Step 13. Cut two 7 1/4" x 7 1/4" squares white solid; cut each square in half on one diagonal to make F corner triangles.

Step 14. Arrange the pieced blocks with the D squares and E and F triangles in diagonal rows as shown in Figure 9; join in rows. Join the rows to complete the pieced top.

Figure 9
Arrange the pieced blocks with the D squares and E and F triangles in diagonal rows.

Step 15. Mark the quilting designs given on the D, E and F pieces referring to Figure 10 for placement on D squares.

Step 16. Sandwich batting between the completed top and prepared backing piece; pin or baste layers together to hold flat.

Figure 10
Mark quilting design on D squares.

Step 17. Quilt as desired by hand or machine. ***Note:** The*

Snowball & Nine-Patch Antique Quilt
Placement Diagram
63 3/4" x 76 1/2"

quilt shown was hand-quilted in the patterns given using white hand-quilting thread.

Step 18. Cut seven 2 1/4" by fabric width strips white solid. Join the strips on short ends to make one long strip for binding.

Step 19. Fold binding strip with wrong sides together along length and press. Pin to the quilt top edges with raw edges even. Stitch all around, mitering corners and overlapping ends. Turn binding to the backside; hand-stitch in place to finish. ❖

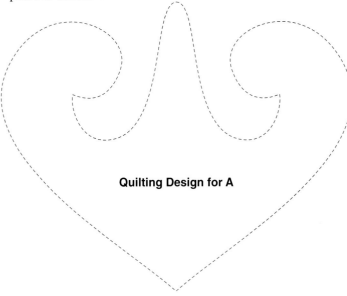

Quilting Design for A

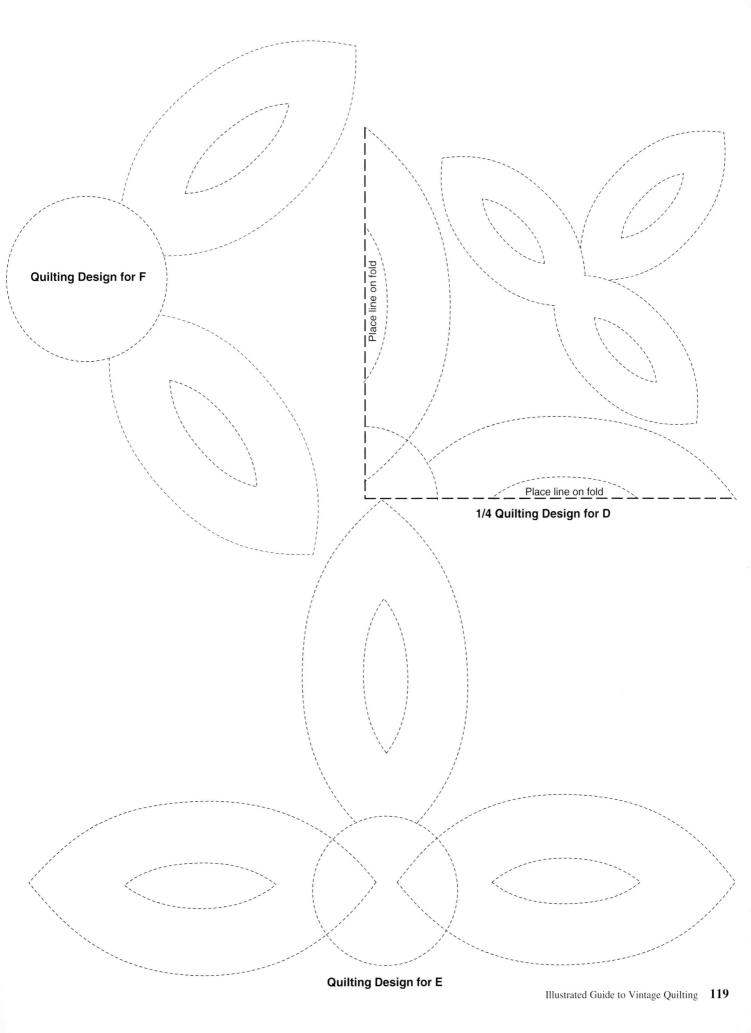

Quilting Design for F

Place line on fold

Place line on fold

1/4 Quilting Design for D

Quilting Design for E

Snowball Bunnies

The Snowball and Nine-Patch blocks are lost in the busy prints used in this simple little crib quilt.

PROJECT NOTES

The antique version of the *Snowball & Nine-Patch* quilt is made with only two fabrics—orange and white. The only design is created by the colored fabric pieces and easily seen. In this quilt, the same design is lost because the print fabrics are so busy.

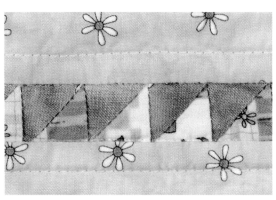

I decided to save the little triangles that were cut off when constructing the Snowball blocks. These little triangles finished at 3/4" when stitched together. I inserted them into the side borders as an accent. They worked perfectly to break up the plain fabric borders.

My fellow quilters tease me because I save such small pieces from my projects. I thought it would be fun to show them that even the tiniest of pieces can be used.

PROJECT SPECIFICATIONS

Quilt Size: 34 1/2" x 43 1/2"

Block Size: 9" x 9"

Number of Blocks: 12

MATERIALS

- 5/8 yard pink/check print
- 5/8 yard yellow print
- 1 yard bunny novelty print
- 1 1/4 yards blue print
- Backing 39" x 48"
- Batting 39" x 48"
- Neutral color all-purpose thread
- Yellow machine-quilting thread
- Clear nylon monofilament
- Basic sewing supplies and tools, rotary cutter, mat and ruler

Snowball & Nine-Patch
9" x 9" Block

INSTRUCTIONS

Step 1. Cut 24 squares bunny novelty print 5" x 5" for A.

Note: The squares in the sample quilt were fussy-cut to place one bunny or plant motif in each square.

Step 2. Cut five strips 2" by fabric width blue print; sub-cut strips into 2" square segments for B. You will need 96 B squares. Draw a diagonal line from corner to corner on the wrong side of each B square.

Step 3. Place a B square right sides together on one corner of A as shown in Figure 1; stitch on the marked line.

Figure 1
Place a B square right sides together on 1 corner of A.

Figure 2
Trim seam to 1/4"; press B to the right side.

Figure 3
Sew B on each corner of A to complete an A-B Snowball unit.

Step 4. Trim seam to 1/4"; press B to the right side as shown in Figure 2. Repeat on each corner of A to complete an A-B Snowball unit as shown in Figure 3. Repeat to make 24 A-B Snowball units. *Note: Save all trimmed and layered triangles for the borders.*

Step 5. Cut seven strips blue print and eight strips pink/check print 2" by fabric width.

Step 6. Sew a blue print strip between two pink/check print strips with right sides together along length to make a pink/blue/pink strip set; press seams toward the blue print strip. Repeat for three pink/blue/pink strip sets.

Step 7. Sew a pink/check print strip between two blue print strips with right sides together along length to make a blue/pink/blue strip set; press seams toward the blue print strips. Repeat for two strip sets.

Step 8. Subcut strip sets into 2" segments as shown in Figure 4; you will need 48 pink/blue/pink and 24 blue/pink/blue segments.

Figure 4
Subcut strip sets into 2" segments.

Figure 5
Join segments to make a Nine-Patch unit.

Step 9. Sew a blue/pink/blue segment between two pink/blue/pink segments to make a Nine-Patch unit as shown in Figure 5; repeat for 24 Nine-Patch units.

Step 10. Sew a Nine-Patch unit to an A-B Snowball unit as shown in Figure 6; repeat. Join the units to complete one Snowball & Nine-Patch block as shown in Figure 7. *Note: If using a one-way design, be sure all designs are stitched together in an upright position.* Repeat for 12 blocks.

Figure 6
Sew a Nine-Patch unit to an A-B Snowball unit.

Figure 7
Join units to complete 1 block.

Step 11. Join three blocks to make a row; press seams in one direction. Repeat for four rows; press seams in one direction.

Step 12. Cut two strips each 2" x 36 1/2" and 2" x 30 1/2" yellow print. Sew the longer strips to opposite sides and shorter strips to the top and bottom of the pieced center; press seams toward strips.

Step 13. Sew the diagonal seams on each layered triangle pair set aside in Step 4 to make triangle/square units as shown in Figure 8. You will need 88 units.

Figure 8
Make triangle/square units as shown.

Figure 9
Join 24 triangle/square units to make a strip.

Step 14. Join 24 triangle/square units to make a strip as shown in Figure 9; repeat for two strips with 24 units each and two strips with 20 units each. Press seams in one direction.

Step 15. Cut two 1 1/4" by fabric width strips blue print; cut strips to make four 1 1/4" x 12" and four 1 1/4" x 9" strips. Sew the longer strips to opposite ends of each 24-unit strip as shown in Figure 10; sew the shorter strips to opposite ends of each 20-unit strip, again referring to Figure 10.

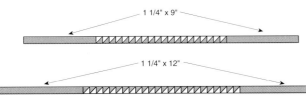

1 1/4" x 9"

1 1/4" x 12"

Figure 10
Sew the 1 1/4" x 12 1/2" strips to opposite ends of a 24-unit strip and the 1 1/4" x 9" strips to the 20-unit strip.

Step 16. Center the longer strips on opposite long sides of the pieced center and stitch. Press seams toward yellow print border strips; trim excess blue print strip at each end.

1 1/2" x 34 1/2"
1 1/2" x 30"
1 1/2" x 40 1/2"
1 1/2" x 36"

Snowball Bunnies
Placement Diagram
34 1/2" x 43 1/2"

Repeat with the shorter strips on the top and bottom of the pieced center.

Step 17. Cut and piece two strips each 2" x 35" and 2" x 41" yellow print. Sew the longer strips to opposite sides and shorter strips to the top and bottom of the pieced center; press seams toward strips.

Step 18. Sandwich batting between the completed top and prepared backing piece; pin or baste layers together to hold flat.

Step 19. Quilt as desired by hand or machine. *Note: The quilt shown was machine-quilted in a meandering design on the blocks using clear nylon monofilament in the top of the machine and all-purpose thread in the bobbin. The borders were machine-quilted in the ditch and 3/8" from seams using yellow machine-quilting thread.*

Step 20. Cut five 2 1/4" by fabric width strips blue print. Join the strips on short ends to make one long strip for binding.

Step 21. Fold binding strip with wrong sides together along length and press. Pin to the quilt top edges with raw edges even. Stitch all around, mitering corners and overlapping ends. Turn binding to the backside; hand-stitch in place to finish. ❖

Sawtooth Medallion Antique Quilt

Many antique quilts are made with white and just one other color.
That contrast is what makes this quilt striking.

PROJECT NOTES

The binding on this old Sawtooth Medallion is worn to shreds on the edges. It needs to be replaced. That would be easy to do—simply make a binding strip a little wider than normal and sew it on right over the old one. There is also a hole from the front right through to the back. This can be mended to look almost like it is part of the original, at least from the front side.

Begin on the backside by cutting a patch 1" larger than the hole all around. Turn under the edges of the patch 1/4" and press. Pin over hole on the backside and hand-stitch in place using thread to match the backing fabrics.

Examine the batting inside the quilt. Using scraps of batting in the same color as that used in the quilt, cut a piece or several pieces of batting to create the same thickness as the original. Slip the batting piece or pieces inside the hole over the area patched from the backside. Pin in place from the backing side.

Determine the shape of the front hole; if it passes through two different fabric colors or pieces, two new pieces should be attached to replace it. Cut fabric patch or patches to fit the size needed plus 1/4" all around. Turn under the edges of the patch and pin in place over the hole; hand-stitch in place, trying to keep the patch stitches as inconspicuous and possible.

The problems with this antique quilt should be taken care of before the quilt can be safely used. This quilt was washed in the machine many times to create such a battered binding. The hole appears to have been caused by catching on some sharp object. When not repaired right away, it grew.

I cannot guess at the age of this quilt. The condition would make it seem old, but I cannot clearly identify the red-and-white print in a time period. The pattern was first printed at the turn of the century.

PROJECT SPECIFICATIONS

Quilt Size: 72" x 84"

Block Size: 8" x 8"

Number of Blocks: 36

MATERIALS

- 3 3/4 yards red-and-white print
- 4 1/2 yards white solid
- Backing 76" x 88"
- Batting 76" x 88"
- Neutral color all-purpose thread
- White hand-quilting thread
- Basic sewing supplies and tools, rotary cutter, mat and ruler

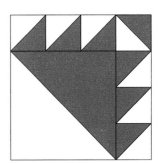

Sawtooth
8" x 8" Block

INSTRUCTIONS

Step 1. Cut 18 squares white solid and 36 squares red-and-white print 6 7/8" x 6 7/8"; cut each square in half on one diagonal to make A triangles. You will need 36 white solid and 72 red-and-white print A triangles.

Step 2. Sew a white solid A to a red-and-white print A as shown in Figure 1 to make an A unit; repeat for 36 A units. Set aside remaining A pieces.

Figure 1
Sew a white solid A to a red-and-white print A.

Step 3. Cut 24 strips 2 7/8" by fabric width each white solid and red-and-white print. Subcut each strip into 2 7/8" segments for B; you will need 328 B squares. Cut each B square in half on one diagonal to make B triangles. You will need 656 B triangles of each fabric.

Step 4. Sew a red-and-white print triangle to a white solid triangle as shown in Figure 2 to make a B unit; repeat for 328 B units. Set aside 152 B units for borders.

Figure 2
Sew a red-and-white print B triangle to a white solid B triangle to make a B unit.

Figure 3
Join 3 B units to make a B3 unit.

Step 5. Join three B units to make a B3 unit as shown in Figure 3; repeat for 72 B3 units.

Step 6. Join four B units to make a B4 unit as shown in Figure 4; repeat for 72 B4 units.

Figure 4
Join 4 B units to make a B4 unit.

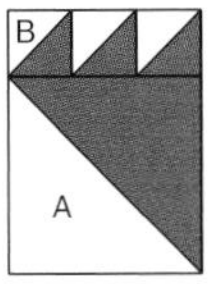

Figure 5
Sew a B3 unit to the red side of an A unit.

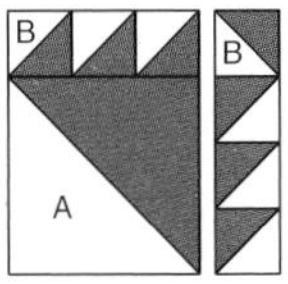

Figure 6
Sew a B4 unit to the remaining red side of the unit to complete 1 block.

Step 7. Sew a B3 unit to the red side of an A unit as shown in Figure 5.

Step 8. Sew a B4 unit to the remaining red side of the A unit as shown in Figure 6 to complete one block; repeat for 36 blocks. Press seams toward B units.

Step 9. Cut four 13 1/4" x 13 1/4" squares white solid; cut each square in half on both diagonals to make C triangles. You will need 16 C triangles.

Step 10. Sew A to adjacent angled sides of a C triangle as shown in Figure 7; press seams toward A.

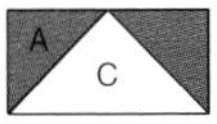

Figure 7
Sew A to adjacent sides of C.

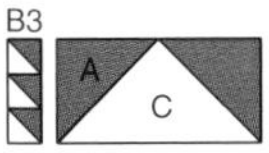

Figure 8
Sew a B3 unit to 1 red end of A-C.

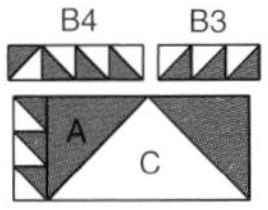

Figure 9
Sew a B3 unit to a B4 unit; sew to the A-B-C unit.

Step 11. Sew a B3 unit to one red end of A-C as shown in Figure 8.

Step 12. Sew a B3 unit to a B4 unit on short white ends as shown in Figure 9; sew to the red long side of A-B-C, again referring to Figure 9.

Step 13. Sew a B4 unit to the remaining red end of the pieced unit to complete one C unit as shown in Figure 10; repeat for 16 C units.

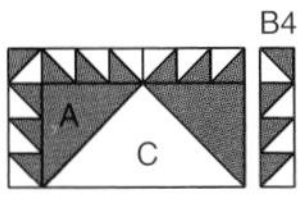

Figure 10
Add a B4 unit to complete the C unit.

Step 14. Cut one 9" x 9" square white solid for D.

Step 15. Sew A to each side of D; press seams toward A.

Step 16. Sew a B3 unit to a B4 unit on short white ends to make a B strip; repeat for four B strips.

Step 17. Sew a B strip to each side of A-D to make a D unit as shown in Figure 11, beginning with a partial seam and ending by completing the partial seam.

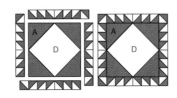

Figure 11
Complete the D unit as shown.

Step 18. Cut six 12 5/8" x

Sawtooth Medallion Antique Quilt
Placement Diagram
72" x 84"

12 5/8" squares white solid; cut each square on both diagonals to make E triangles. You will need 22 E triangles.

Step 19. Cut two 6 5/8" x 6 5/8" squares white solid; cut each square on one diagonal to make F triangles. You will need four F triangles.

Step 20. Arrange the blocks in diagonal rows with the C and D units and the E and F triangles as shown in Figure 12;

Figure 12
Arrange blocks, C and D units and E and F triangles in diagonal rows.

Continued on page 128

Black & White Sawtooth

The Sawtooth block design makes a bold statement in this updated version made with black-and-white prints.

PROJECT NOTES

The original antique version of this block was made with only two colors—red and white. The layout of that quilt (see page 123) was entirely different than the layout of this modern counterpart. Even though the newer version only uses two colors—black and white—the graphic layout creates a whole new look for this classic old design. Because the block has been expanded to include Flying Geese units instead of triangle/square units, I have referred to only the center of this project as the block—Broken Dishes. Figure 1 highlights the original block in this arrangement. You can see that by making one small change, a completely different block is created.

Figure 1
The original Sawtooth block is highlighted in red in this drawing.

PROJECT SPECIFICATIONS

Quilt Size: 48" x 48"

Block Size: 12" x 12"

Number of Blocks: 4

MATERIALS

- 1/4 yard black solid
- 3/4 yard total 3 different black-with-white prints
- 3/4 yard black-and-white stripe
- 1 3/4 yards white-with-black print
- Backing 52" x 52"
- Batting 52" x 52"
- Black and white all-purpose thread
- Black machine-quilting thread
- Basic sewing supplies and tools, rotary cutter, mat and ruler

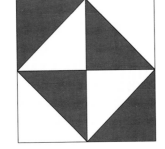

Broken Dishes
12" x 12" Block

INSTRUCTIONS

Step 1. Cut eight 6 7/8" x 6 7/8" squares each white-with-black and black-with-white prints. Cut each square in half on one diagonal for A triangles. You will need 16 A triangles of each color.

Step 2. Sew a white-with-black A to a black-with-white A to make an A unit as shown in Figure 2; repeat for 16 A units.

Figure 2
Sew a white-with-black A to a black-with-white A to make an A unit.

Step 3. Join two A units as shown in Figure 3; repeat for eight units.

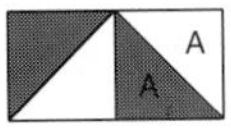

Step 4. Join two of the A-A units to complete one block as shown in Figure 4; repeat for four blocks. Set aside.

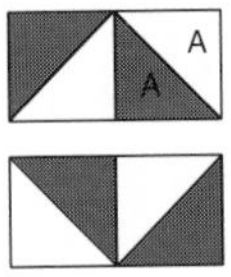

Figure 3
Join 2 A units.

Figure 4
Join 2 of the A-A units to complete 1 block.

Step 5. Cut ten 4 1/2" by fabric width strips white-with-black print; subcut each strip into 2 1/2" segments for B. You will need 152 B rectangles.

Step 6. Cut 19 strips 2 1/2" by fabric width from the black-with-white prints. Subcut each strip into 2 1/2" square segments for C; you will need 304 C squares. Draw a diagonal line from corner to corner on the wrong side of each C square.

Step 7. Place a C square on one corner of B and stitch on drawn line as shown in Figure 5; trim seam to 1/4" and press to the right side as shown in Figure 6. Repeat on the opposite end of B to complete a B-C unit as shown in Figure 7; repeat for 152 B-C units.

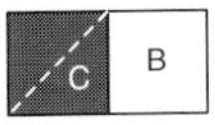

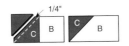

Figure 5
Place a C square on 1 corner of B and stitch on drawn line.

Figure 6
Trim seam to 1/4" and press to the right side.

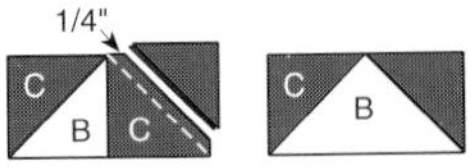

Figure 7
Complete the B-C unit as shown.

Step 8. Join three B-C units as shown in Figure 8; repeat for 24 B-C3 units. Press seams in one direction.

Step 9. Join two B-C3 units to make a B-C6 unit as shown in Figure 9; repeat for 12 B-C6 units.

Figure 8
Join 3 B-C units to make a B-C3 unit.

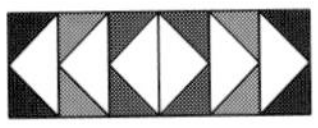

Figure 9
Join 2 B-C3 units to make a B-C6 unit.

Figure 10
Join 2 blocks with 3 B-C6 units to make a block row.

Step 10. Join two blocks with three B-C6 units as shown in Figure 10 to make a block row; repeat for two block rows. Press seams toward blocks.

Step 11. Cut nine squares black-with-white print 4 1/2" x

4 1/2" for D. **Note:** *The quilt would be less busy if these squares are cut from black solid.*

Step 12. Join two B-C6 units with three D squares to make a sashing row as shown in Figure 11; repeat for three sashing rows. Press seams toward D.

Figure 11
Join 2 B-C6 units with 3 D squares to make a sashing row.

Step 13. Join the block rows with the sashing rows to completed the pieced center; press seams toward block rows.

Step 14. Cut two strips each 2 1/2" x 36 1/2" and 2 1/2" x 40 1/2" black-and-white stripe. Sew the shorter strips to the top and bottom and longer strips to opposite sides of the pieced center; press seams toward strips.

Step 15. Join 20 B-C units to make a side border strip as shown in Figure 12; repeat for four strips. Press seams in one direction.

Figure 12
Join 20 B-C units to make a side border strip.

Step 16. Sew a B-C strip to opposite sides of the pieced top, referring to the Placement Diagram for positioning; press seams away from pieced strips. Cut four 4 1/2" x 4 1/2" black solid D squares. Sew a D square to each end of the remaining two strips; sew to the remaining sides of the pieced center, referring to the Placement Diagram. Press seams away from pieced strips.

Step 17. Sandwich batting between the completed top and prepared backing piece; pin or baste layers together to hold flat.

Step 18. Quilt as desired by hand or machine. **Note:** *The quilt shown was machine-quilted in the ditch of the dark A pieces, in straight lines between blocks and border strips*

Black & White Sawtooth
Placement Diagram
48" x 48"

and in a straight line through the center of each B-C unit in the border using black machine-quilting thread.

Step 19. Cut five 2 1/4" by fabric width strips black-and-white stripe. Join the strips on short ends to make one long strip for binding.

Step 20. Fold binding strip with wrong sides together along length and press. Pin to the quilt top edges with raw edges even. Stitch all around, mitering corners and overlapping ends. Turn binding to the backside; hand-stitch in place to finish. ❖

Sawtooth Medallion Antique Quilt
Continued from page 125

join in rows. Join rows to complete the pieced center; press seams in one direction.

Step 21. Join 40 B units referring to the Placement Diagram to make a side border strip. **Note:** *The sides should measure 80 1/8" at this point and 40 units measures 80 1/2". The pieced top will stretch the 3/8" difference between the two measurements to fit an even number of B units. Otherwise, either a strip would need to be added to make an even size, or a very strange size B unit would have to be pieced.*

Step 22. Sew a 40-unit B strip to opposite long sides of the pieced center; press seams toward strips.

Step 23. Join 36 B units referring to the Placement Diagram to make the top and bottom border strips. Sew a strip to the top

and bottom of the pieced center; press seams toward strips.

Step 24. Sandwich batting between the completed top and prepared backing piece; pin or baste layers together to hold flat.

Step 25. Quilt as desired by hand or machine. **Note:** *The quilt shown was hand-quilted in a clamshell design in the A, C, D, E and F pieces and 1/4" from seams in the remaining pieces using white hand-quilting thread.*

Step 26. Cut eight 2 1/4" by fabric width strips red-and-white print. Join the strips on short ends to make one long strip for binding.

Step 27. Fold binding strip with wrong sides together along length and press. Pin to the quilt top edges with raw edges even. Stitch all around, mitering corners and overlapping ends. Turn binding to the backside; hand-stitch in place to finish. ❖

Metric Conversion Charts

Standard Equivalents

U.S. Measurement		Metric Measurement		
1/8 inch	=	3.20 mm	=	0.32 cm
1/4 inch	=	6.35 mm	=	0.635 cm
3/8 inch	=	9.50 mm	=	0.95 cm
1/2 inch	=	12.70 mm	=	1.27 cm
5/8 inch	=	15.90 mm	=	1.59 cm
3/4 inch	=	19.10 mm	=	1.91 cm
7/8 inch	=	22.20 mm	=	2.22 cm
1 inch	=	25.40 mm	=	2.54 cm
1/8 yard	=	11.43 cm	=	0.11 m
1/4 yard	=	22.86 cm	=	0.23 m
3/8 yard	=	34.29 cm	=	0.34 m
1/2 yard	=	45.72 cm	=	0.46 m
5/8 yard	=	57.15 cm	=	0.57 m
3/4 yard	=	68.58 cm	=	0.69 m
7/8 yard	=	80.00 cm	=	0.80 m
1 yard	=	91.44 cm	=	0.91 m

Metric Conversions

U.S. Measurements		Multiplied by		Metric Measurement
yards	x	.9144	=	meters (m)
yards	x	91.44	=	centimeters (cm)
inches	x	2.54	=	centimeters (cm)
inches	x	25.4	=	millimeters (mm)
inches	x	.0254	=	meters (m)

Metric Measurements		Multiplied by		U.S. Measurements
centimeters	x	.3937	=	inches
meters	x	1.0936	=	yards

Embroidery Stitch Guide

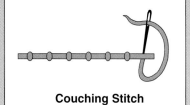
Buttonhole Stitch

French Knot

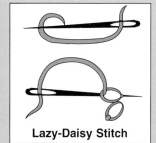
Lazy-Daisy Stitch

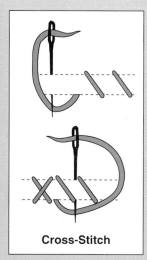
Cross-Stitch

Couching Stitch

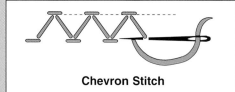
Chevron Stitch

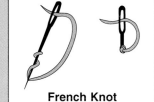
Herringbone Stitch

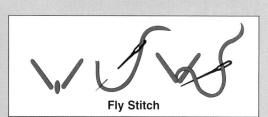
Fly Stitch

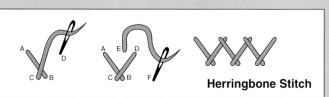
Feather Stitches

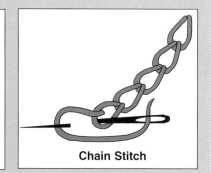
Chain Stitch

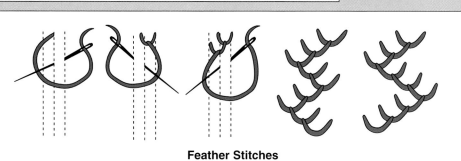

Thank You

We thank the following individuals and companies for helping us with this book.

Page 23: *Double X Bag*—Machine-pieced and machine-quilted by Sue Harvey.

Page 42: *Plaid Mystery Foot Warmer*—Hobbs Organic Cotton Batting and Mission Valley Homespuns.

Page 64: *Tulip Pillowcases*—Aunt Grace fabric collection from Marcus Brothers. Tulip appliqué stitched by Sue Harvey.

Page 75: *Colonial Basket Pillow Shams*—Baltimore Album fabric collection by Judie Rothermel from Marcus Brothers and Mountain Mist Gold cotton polyester batting.

Page 99: *Mrs. Brown's Choice Table Runner*—Judy's Indigo fabric collection by Judy Rothermel from Marcus Brothers.

Page 104: *Shadow Star Table Topper*—Cotton cord from Conso.

Page 112: *Sunflower Stars*—Bountiful Harvest and Charleston Gardens fabric collections from Northcott/Monarch Silks and Hobbs Heirloom Organic cotton batting. Machine-quilted by Dianne Hodgkins.

Page 120: *Snowball Bunnies*—The Hatfields fabric collection by Sharon Reynolds of Tenderberry Stitches for Northcott/Monarch Silks and Mountain Mist White Gold Iron-on 100 percent cotton batting.

Page 126: *Black & White Sawtooth*—Bright Bits prints from Marcus Brothers.